28th ASIA-PACIFIC INTERIOR DESIGN AWARDS

APIDA

ARTPOWER

28th ASIA-PACIFIC INTERIOR DESIGN AWARDS
© Artpower International Publishing Co., Ltd.

ACS1   ARTPOWER

Edited and produced by Artpower International Publishing Co., Ltd.
Address: Flat B5 1/F, Manning Ind. Bldg., 116-118 How Ming St., Kwun Tong, Kowloon, Hong Kong, China
Tel: 852-23977886
Fax: 852-23982111

www.artpower.com.cn
contact@artpower.com.cn (Editorial)
book@artpower.com.cn (Sales - China)
overseasales@artpower.com.cn (Sales - International)

ISBN 978-988-75070-1-7

Publisher: Lu Jican
Chief Editor: Wang Chen
Executive Editor: Huang Yujia
Art Designer: Chen Ting
Cover Design: Xiong Libo

Size: 248mm X 290mm
First Edition: Feburary, 2022

All Rights Reserved. No part of this publication may be reproduced or utilised in any form by any means, electronic or mechanical, including photocopying, recording or by any information storage and retrieval system, without prior written permission of the publisher.

All images in this book have been reproduced with the knowledge and prior consent of the designers and the clients concerned, and every effort has been made to ensure that credits accurately comply with information applied. No responsibility is accepted by producer, publisher, or printer for any infringement of copyright or otherwise arising from the contents of this publication.

Printed and bound in China.

PREFACE

Joey Ho
Chairman
Hong Kong Interior Design Association (HKIDA)

The success of APIDA this year is nothing short of a miracle, where adversity brings diversity in ambitious design solutions to take on the biggest challenges of our times.

This is why I'm really excited to notice that, among our entries, and despite all the havoc, everyone has been trying to address and interpret our shifting physical and mental needs more profoundly, and rapidly produce a greater number of ingenious projects than ever.

For example, we can notice this blurring boundary between public and private spaces, and the surge of interesting proposals to re-imagine how we live together. Be it co-living or co-working space, innovative strategies explore our new network of intricate relationships defined by everything from remote working to shared community. Spatially speaking, this rise of 'new normal' has presented new opportunities for us to experiment with more radical ideas.

Pushing new boundaries has always been a creative mission for us designers, and our professionalism can be seen through our committed care for both our patrons and end users, while rising above socio-economic constraints. With that goal in mind, I would like to congratulate all our awardees for their achievements, and to thank all the participants for their support of APIDA in this eventful year.

While all of us at APIDA are immensely grateful for your inspiring submissions, we are also keenly anticipating what is to come next year. Collectively, we can go much further and emerge stronger.

A year full of unprecedented surprises, 2020 has affected everyone in our design industry as much as all our work partners. The impact of the pandemic weighing on all of us has also pushed us to exercise our creative prowess more than ever beyond our projects, including all of us organising APIDA.

Despite all the challenges, we are becoming stronger than ever and going digital for the first time all the way from entry submission to award presentation. This would not have been possible without the unwavering support from designers all over Asia, and the prestige we have built around APIDA throughout the years.

We are immensely grateful to receive their diverse submissions, and to all the judges and committee members for pulling off an extraordinary feat in keeping everything in place. Nothing is impossible and nothing can stop us celebrating design excellence which can truly make a positive impact on our lives, especially at this critical moment.

Congratulations to all the well-deserved winners. Take care and see you around next year.

Enoch Hui
Chairman of Organizing Committee
Asia Pacific Interior Design Awards (APIDA)

008
HONG KONG INTERIOR DESIGN
ASSOCIATION (HKIDA)

010
ASIA-PACIFIC INTERIOR DESIGN
AWARDS (APIDA)

013
JUDGE'S PROFILE

019
JUDGE'S CHOICE

033
HONG KONG BEST AWARD

 043
FOOD SPACE

 077
INSTALLATION & EXHIBITION SPACE

109
LEISURE & ENTERTAINMENT SPACE

 147
INSTITUTIONAL SPACE

185
SHOPPING SPACE

 217
HOTEL SPACE

 251
SAMPLE SPACE

 289
LIVING SPACE

 319
SMALL LIVING SPACE

 351
WORK SPACE

 385
SMALL WORK SPACE

 421
STUDENT

FOOD SPACE

044
Nana's Green Tea Eias in Okinawa Toyosaki

050
Shang Thai

056
HEYTEA LAB at the MixC Xiamen

062
The Unity of Zen and Martial Arts

068
WU

INSTALLATION & EXHIBITION SPACE

078
Aranya Art Center

084
UTTER SPACE

090
Yingliang Stone Natural History Museum

096
Newton and Moon

102
Artizon Museum

LEISURE & ENTERTAINMENT SPACE

110
Exhibition of Frozen Time

116
Xi'an Changjiang Insun Cinema

122
Changsha Insun International Cinema

128
Sanshui Cultural Centre

134
TaiOursea SPA Shop

140
Backstage Glory

INSTITUTIONAL SPACE

148
Enjoy the Time

154
Reading Under the Lake

160
Thetford Kindergarden

166
WuliEpoch Culture Centre

172
Interior Renovation of the 4th Building of Tsinghua University

178
Tiny Doo Doo Pediatric Clinic

SHOPPING SPACE

186
K11 Musea

192
Holiland Concept Store

198
Magic Box

204
Majimaya Confectionery Tool Shop

210
Muse Edition

HOTEL SPACE

218
Kimpton Da An Hotel

224
Sincere Hotel

230
The Sukhothai Shanghai

236
Hotel Anteroom Naha

244
The Westin in Zhongshan

SAMPLE SPACE

252
Obsidian Villa

258
Silent

264
The Entrance

270
Jiangshan Wanli Aerial Villa

276
Connaught Serviced Apartments

282
Sunac Elegant West Garden

LIVING SPACE

290
Sanctuary of the Soul

296
The Home for a Brand New Start

302
Grosvenor Residence

306
House in Minohshinmachi

312
Mount Pavilia

SMALL LIVING SPACE

320
Axis House

326
Layers

332
La Parfumeuse

338
Savour Dwelling

344
Between Mountains and Sea

WORK SPACE

352
Xige Estate

358
Poly Raise Space

364
The PolyCuboid Office Building

370
C&C Design Co,. Ltd. Creative Headquarters

378
YIJING Architecture Design Studio

SMALL WORK SPACE

386
MGY Base

392
RMA Office

398
Encounter

404
Mastermind JAPAN Office

410
Release

416
Lou Bai (Liu Bai)

STUDENT

422
Rebuilding Communication — Tower of Babel

428
Nirvana

436
Buddhismscraper in Tibet

442
Shell Plaza

HONG KONG INTERIOR DESIGN ASSOCIATION (HKIDA)

ABOUT HKIDA

Hong Kong Interior Design Association (HKIDA) is a non-governmental and non-profit organisation founded in 1991. Throughout the years, our members have grown to include a vibrant community of interior designers, contractors, suppliers, students and other professional practitioners in the field of interior architecture.

HKIDA is devoted to serve the needs of our members, industry partners and the general public. One of our major undertakings has been fostering professionalism and design excellence. This includes a comprehensive development of the elaborate codes of conduct, innovation on both creative and technical fronts, as well as the celebration of craftsmanship. HKIDA actively engages in research and education, initiates regional competitions and organises activities which invites participation on a broader social level.

Our success relies on the ongoing industry support and recognition. HKIDA works closely with various associations, academics and professionals from commercial and public sectors to further realise our goals and commitment to outstanding interior designs and designers - and for the benefit of all.

Member of

 International Federation of Interior Architects/Designers

 APSDA
Asia-Pacific Space Designers Association

AIMS OF HKIDA

1. Gathering Point
HKIDA brings together design and project talents to benefit both businesses and consumers.

2. Education Facilitator
Through on-going training and education programmes, we develop knowledge of excellence in design, construction and overall project quality.

3. Industry Hub
We continue to develop and improve professional standards of designers, contractors and suppliers with an updated codes of conduct, while keeping up with the standards of creativity, workmanship and technical innovation.

4. Standard Torchbearer
Throughout the design and construction of the interior environment, HKIDA seeks to promote awareness of public health and safety and the implementation of new technical knowledge and materials.

5. Professional Recognition
Our standards of professionalism, codes of ethics and business practices are welcomed by members of the industry and their clients alike as satisfied customers.

6. Information Network
We always channel and archive useful information on our community with our members through exhibitions, seminars and other supporting activities.

7. Exchange Platform
We facilitate the flow of ideas and information amongst designers, contractors, suppliers and the public both in Hong Kong and internationally, while catering to their different needs.

8. Green Innovator
We are devoted to R&D projects relating to the use of environmentally-friendly products and the promotion of these products.

9. Collaboration Advocate
By furthering our affiliation worldwide with international organisations, we hope to inspire sustainable collaborations to bring mutual benefits.

10. Quality Reassurance
We strive to help our members to gain recognition from the governing authorities and public at large, while enlightening the public as to the importance of employing qualified professionals.

ASIA-PACIFIC INTERIOR DESIGN AWARDS (APIDA)

ASIA-PACIFIC INTERIOR DESIGN AWARDS (APIDA)

As the signature event of HKIDA, APIDA aims to recognise outstanding interior design projects and designers, and promote professional standards and ethics among interior design practices. Open to all design professionals all over the world. APIDA is an excellent opportunity for interior designers in the region to gain worldwide recognition and public acclaim.

OBJECTIVE

- Enhance public awareness of interior design as an important aspect of everyday life;
- Acknowledge and give industry recognition to quality projects and designers;
- Encourage and promote professional standards and ethics among interior design practices operating in the region.

APIDA CRITERIA

1. Originality and Innovation
2. Functionality
3. Space Planning
4. Aesthetics

CATEGORIES

1. Food Space
Cafes, bars, lounges, restaurants, canteens, food courts. etc.

2. Installation & Exhibition Space
Gallery, museum, trade exhibitions, sales offices provided by realty developers, art installations, public park installation, etc.

3. Leisure & Entertainment Space
Spas, swimming pools, clubs, cinemas/theatres, health/fitness centres, gyms, beauty centres, salon, game centres, theme park, etc.

4. Institutional Space
Community centres, schools, kids playgroups, education/learning centres, libraries, hospitals, clinics, airports, public transport stations, government space, etc.

5. Shopping Space
Shops, retail outlets, showrooms, department stores, food markets, shopping malls, kiosks, etc.

6. Hotel Space
Commercial hotels, budget hotels, city hotels, resort, service apartments, etc.

7. Sample Space
Show flat provided by realty developers to create an environment on actual building site or offsite prototype to promote the sales of the property.

8. Living Space
Apartments, private houses, etc. (139 m^2 or above)

9. Small Living Space
Apartments, private houses, housing developments, etc. (less than 139 m^2)

10. Work Space
Offices, studios, warehouses, factories, co-working space, etc. (278 m^2 or above)

11. Small Work Space
Reception areas, offices, studios, warehouses, factories, co-working space, etc. (less than 278 m^2)

12. Student
Design projects submitted by interior design / interior architecture students.

JUDGE'S PROFILE

Jurgen Bey
Founder & Director
Studio Makkink & Bey

In 2002 design office Studio Makkink & Bey was founded by Rianne Makkink (1964) and Jurgen Bey (1965). In their eyes, urban planning, architecture and landscape architecture are inextricably connected to product design. The light bulb influenced architecture, the constructed house has formed the household interior and skyscrapers could never have existed without the elevator. In more than 300 projects, commissioned by museums, galleries, art or government organizations, companies and private commissioners, as well as in many lectures a design vision is delivered in which the form of a design follows from its context.

Studio Makkink & Bey develops products on a small scale, such as furniture and tableware, interiors of private houses, museums, offices and other public spaces. The larger scale of architecture and urbanism is addressed in the design of various pavilions, parks and studies into new ways to program areas. Each time a design by Studio Makkink & Bey starts with constructing a story based on what already exists such as functions, structures and objects. Networking and systematic thinking allows to create connections between context, objects and functions. Through sharp analysis and programming, the potential of a district, a building or product is optimally put to use. The study repertoire includes the consumption of energy and raw materials, dual-use, food production, social and economic systems. An example is for instance the study of the informal economy that are present in India in order to find answers to economic problems in Europe.

David Frank
Design Director -Senior Associate
Gensler

With more than 20 years of professional experience, David has built a diverse portfolio of innovative workplace interiors for companies such as Belkin, Edelman, JP Morgan Chase, Yahoo! and EY as well as public spaces for Chinese developers such as Vanke and Kerry Properties.

As a Design Director at Gensler Hong Kong, David specializes in workplace design and strategy, overseeing the design of corporate, commercial, technology, and public space projects in Hong Kong and Mainland China.

He believes in crafting authentic design solutions unique to each project's aspirations. He adopts a design thinking approach to deliver spaces that inspire and engage users, while solving complex business problems.

David's work has been published in trade magazines such as *Interior Design Magazine, Interiors & Sources, Korean Interiors* and website Office Snapshots as well as multiple award nominations for *Interior Design Magazine* "Best of the Year Award" and IIDA Southern California chapter's annual "Calibre Design Awards" and he is often sought after for design industry speaking events and judging panels.

Joey Ho
Chairman
Hong Kong Interior Design Association

Joey Ho draws his creative inspiration from the far-reaching corners of Asia. Born in Taiwan, raised in Singapore, graduated from The University of Hong Kong (Master of Architecture) and The National University of Singapore (Bachelor of Architectural Studies). Each of these culturally diverse yet artistically vibrant qualities have played their part in fashioning Joey's unique and avant-garde perspectives of the world. Joey has established a high profile clientele in corporate, residential, education, hospitality and various sectors, with projects over Hong Kong, the Greater China region, Singapore, India, the US and Australia. To date, Joey's designs have won numerous internationally recognized awards. He is the Chairman of the Hong Kong Interior Design Association, the director of Hong Kong Design Centre, course consultant of Hong Kong Institute of Vocational Education and advisory committee member of Hong Kong Trade and Development Council, actively involved in promoting the development of the design industry.

Shigeru Kubota was born in Tokyo, Japan in 1969 and established Kubota Architects and Associates Inc. in 2003.

Planning, design producing and design works has covered a wide range of categories including architecture, interior, products, and so on. The famous works are The Warehouse, Galaxy Harajuku, Mercedes-Benz Connection, Bosch Café, METoA Ginza(Mitsubishi Electric's Showroom), Tsutaya Tokyo Roppongi, etc. He won many prizes, Mercedes-Benz Connection, Imabari Towel Minamiaoyana, UT(UNIQLO T-Shit Store) and more.

Shigeru Kubota
President
Kubota Architect &Associates Inc.

Born in Hong Kong and raised in London, Emily is an internationally published editor and creative professional with 17 years in the media and publishing industry. Her expertise spans the spectrum of lifestyle, interiors design and people, and she is passionate about producing engaging multimedia that resonates with and inspires readers and brands.

Educated in law from the University of Hong Kong, Emily is currently the Publisher and Editor-In-Chief of *Home Journal* – the authority brand in Asia on interiors and lifestyle. She is responsible for the editorial strategy and brand direction of the company's key products and extensions – *Home Journal*, *Home Solutions* (Design and Decoration Bible), *Home Buyers Guide* (Directory of the Best Sources for the Home), *Transitions* (Curated Guide to the Best Interior Designers) and the Asia Designers Community – as well as overseeing the execution across all their digital platforms.

Emily's ultimate goals are crafting authentic design solutions for businesses and projects, discovering new talent, and advocating the importance and promotion of meaningful design across different

Emily Leung
Publisher
Home Journal

Felix Li
President
The Hong Kong Institute of Architects

Felix Li is a Director with TFP Farrells. Since joining Farrells in 2006, he has been responsible for implementing projects by leading planning/design review, project management and contract administration. He joined The Hong Kong Institute of Architects (HKIA) and Architects Registration Board (ARB) in 1995 and also registered as an Authorized Person in the same year. He obtained the PRC Class 1 Registered Architect Qualification in 2006.

He has been a Fellow of HKIA since 2013 and has been elected as Council of HKIA since 2013. He was the Co-Chair of the Board of Mainland Affairs in 2013, leading the Board to liaise with relevant Mainland government departments and local professional institutes. He led two researches on "Comparison of architect's role in Hong Kong and Mainland" and "The PRC legislation and taxation frameworks for architects practicing in Mainland China". He was the Deputy Chair of the Board of Educational Affairs in 2015 and involved in the HKIA/ARB Professional Assessment and local HKIA/ARB accreditation activities. He was the Vice President of HKIA between 2017-18. He is the current President of The Hong Kong Institute of Architects.

Johnny Lin is responsible for the businesses such as workplace-related interior design and development/brand strategy consultation in China. For more than 30 years, Johnny Lin has delivered project solutions in major international hubs spanning from Asia to the Middle East. Johnny focuses on assuring design, quality control, project delivery, business development and user experience, and provides numerous high-quality works for developers, investors, and enterprises for workplace projects. Currently, he is also the President of the Federal Advisory Council of Hong Kong Real Property Federation.

JUDGE'S CHOICE

Rebuilding Communication — Tower of Babel

School
The Guangzhou Academy of Fine Arts

Project Designers
Huang Xiaobin

Project Location
China

Site Area
400 m²

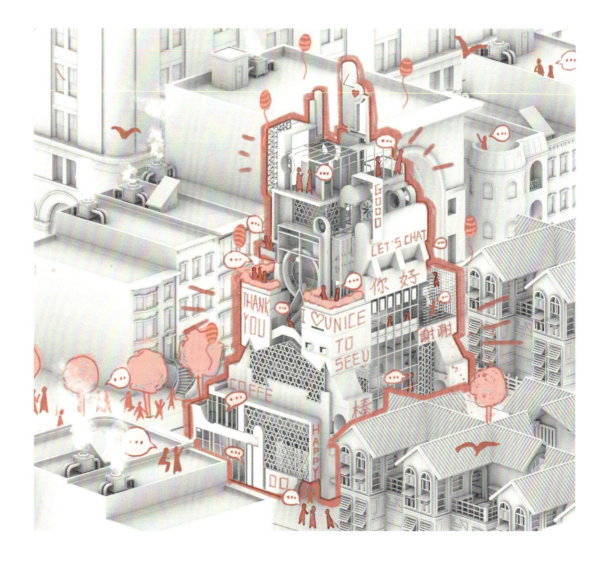

Jurgen Bey
Founder & Director
Studio Makkink & Bey

The whole idea of public space and common ground is so important. Property is such a waste of usage waiting most of the time to be used. We tend to only think in public space on ground floors yet we need to be with more and more people in dense places. It's time that we develop our public spaces also with a view. In the 50's till 70's the highway with its cars and horizons were the promised land of future prosperity and technology. Maybe we should now consider high-rise as the way to develop future and horizon, therefore make the availability of this architecture inclusive and therefore changing percentages into public space. This project refers to that and most projects shown were still addressed mostly to the aesthetics of having and owning.

A Private Fish Maw Museum

Design Company
Jingu Phoenix Space Planning Organization

Project Designers
Ye Hui, Chen Jian, Lin Weibin, Chen Xuexian

Location
China

Site Area
800 m²

David Frank
Design Director - Senior Associate
Gensler

Certainly hard to select a single standout from all the great submissions but one that I really went back to and just caught me off guard was the Private Fish Maw Museum. Personally living in the Sheung Wan area of Hong Kong near our local "dried seafood street" of Wing Lok Street never could I imagine after passing the sights and smells of the many street shops daily, seeing fish maw as something experienced in the Private Fish Maw Museum. The elegance and artistic expression of the space and the crafted journey of storytelling changed my whole perception of how something I saw as a basic food ingredient and not at all glamorous or high end, is valued and important to a people and culture and the process of its production a tradition and craft.

Judge's Choice

Shopping Space

K11 Musea

Design Company
New World Development Company Limited

Project Designers
Collaborate with AB concept, KPF, Laab & Speirs and Major

Location
Hong Kong, China

Site Area
30,000 m²

Joey Ho
Chairman
Hong Kong Interior Design Association

In this age of online shopping, designing shopping malls with memorable effects is nothing short of a challenge. An engineering feat is the 35m-high atrium of K11 Musea, dubbed Opera Theatre, featuring 1,800 programmable spotlights across the ceiling. However, APIDA judges have always been looking for trend-setting concepts beyond visual appeal. Here, the developer has consciously decided to rise above simply "buy and sell" creating a public forum for cultural and social exchanges, and incentivizing visitors to return time after time.

We all know that relying merely on designers working hard is not enough. We appreciate their engagement of both local and international design talent in the project, and their support for experimentation and collaboration.

I would like to congratulate everyone who has contributed to the successful design of K11 Musea, and their ongoing effort in keeping alive this synergy among art, culture and design.

FELIX LI
President
The Hong Kong Institute of Architects

The shopping mall displays a high level of design and implementation quality. The artisan style design throughout the whole circulation/landlord areas sets the theme for the new shopping icon for Hong Kong and may as well Asia. The elegant design of the public and circulation areas provides the general public and shoppers a brand-new shopping experience and wonderful journey to the shops or even just pass-by.

The use of material and its workmanship are thoroughly considered and reflect the efforts of the designers and clients and implementation team. Architects and designers and co-ordinate with all the design teams to achieve the overall design are commendable. The project should be recognized for its design icon around the world and supports to the overall and HK design professions.

Judge's Choice

Installation & Exhibition Space

Yingliang Stone Natural History Museum

Design Company
Atelier Alter Architects

Project Designers
Jiyuan Zhang, Xiaojun Bu, Zhenwei Li, Jiahe Zhang, Lairong Zheng, Bo Huang, Leilei Ma

Location
Fujian, China

Site Area
2,600 m²

Shigeru Kubota
President
Kubota Architect & Associates Inc.

The scale and the shape of the atrium are marvellous in the large space.The huge rock-like design has the feeling of not only the weight but the lightness to my surprise. I believe this space can offer spatial experience that one has never experienced before, with overwhelming power of every element, such as the combination of high atrium and low ceiling, the unity of material and the light reaching out from the high ceiling opening.

Judge's Choice

Installation & Exhibition Space

Newton and Moon

Design Company
DOMANI Architectural Concepts

Project Designers
Ann Yu

Location
Guangdong, China

Site Area
2,000 m²

Emily Leung
Publisher
Home Journal

This is a particularly stunning and unique commercial space combining balance, proportion, mood and a strong element of surprise. The light and shadow and the mixture of elements throughout the space indeed, ignites all the senses. The theme is also particularly well adapted, with the decentralised free moving line being theconstruction method of the space.

MGY Base

Design Company
teamSTAR

Project Designers
Satake Eitaro

Location
Japan

Site Area
125 m²

Judge's Choice

Small Work Space

Johniny Lin
Vice-President
CallisonRTKL

The full use of small spaces gives a sense of spaciousness and the natural colour palette makes the overall space bright and airy.

HONG KONG BEST AWARD

Hong Kong Best Award

Shopping Space

K11 Musea

Design Company
New World Development Company Limited

Project Designers
Collaborate with AB concept, KPF, Laab & Speirs and Major

Project Location
Hong Kong, China

Site Area
30,000 m²

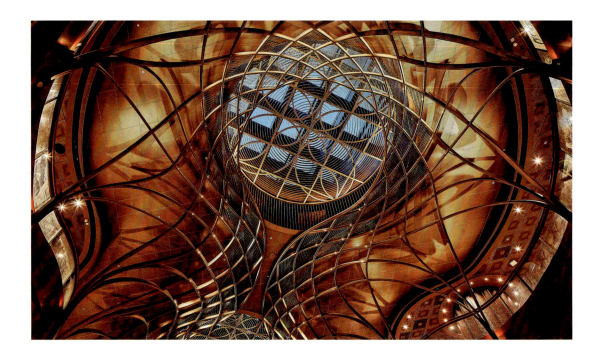

The project is more than just a place to shop; it also highlights culture, art and design. K11 has teamed up with 100 artists from different disciplines and cultures to revitalise the mall and make K11 Musea a cultural Silicon Valley, infusing art, architecture, design, sustainable environmental concepts and culture in all its forms into the daily lives of new consumers.

Inspired by the 'Muse by the Sea', the centrepiece of the mall is a 35-metre high atrium, known as the 'Opera House', which consists of approximately 1,800 programmable spotlights that look like a galaxy, evoking a sense of wonder and creativity in the form of galaxies and mysterious stellar bodies. curiosity and creativity. The elaborate arrangement of lights on the opera-like ceiling creates a 'creative galaxy', with a giant sphere installation acting as a focal point for the audience, further enhancing the illusion that one is looking into space.

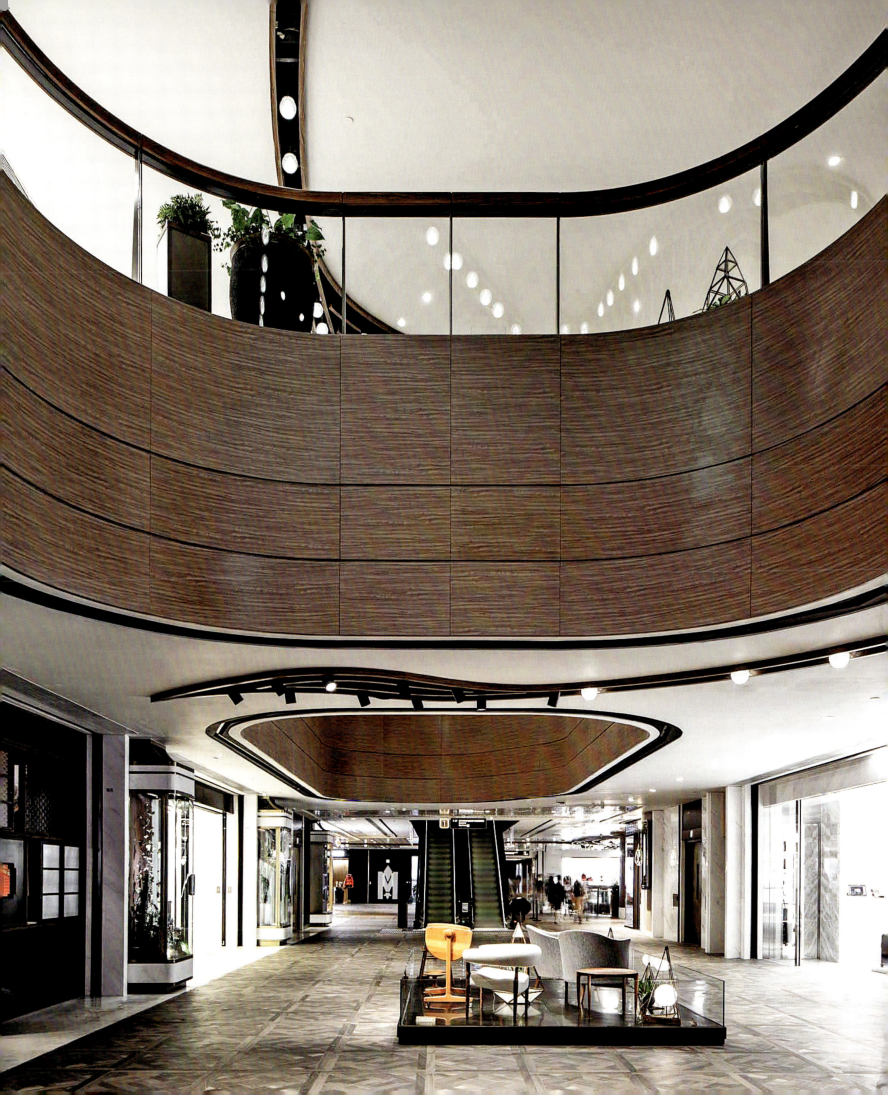

Nana's Green Tea Eias in Okinawa Toyosaki

Design Company
KAMITOPEN Co.,Ltd.

Project Designers
Masahiro Yoshida, Tae Fukaumi, Asuka Tamaru

Project Location
Japan

Site Area
127.8 m²

Nana is a company that is spreading "New Japanese Style" to the world with "Matcha" as its starting point. They offer their customers high quality matcha with a modern menu, such as matcha lattes. Therefore, the focus of the shop design is not "Japanese" but "modern tea room". In the owner's words, he wanted to present "a shop where people can enjoy traditional Japanese tea culture through a modern interpretation". We hope that this shop will create a tea ceremony craze among young people.

In this facade of the town of Toyosaki, Okinawa, you can savour the history of the tea room and have an experience that transcends time if you understand the spirit of the tea room, the spirit of the farshu-ryu tea ceremony, which is the symbolic meaning of the tea room arrangement by the tea ceremony patriarch Rikyu.

The designer painted the walls and ceiling with mortar and drew white lines on them to blur the boundaries between actual objects and pictorial works, creating a sense of 'imagination' and 'reality', thus creating a space that is not bound by the concept of time.

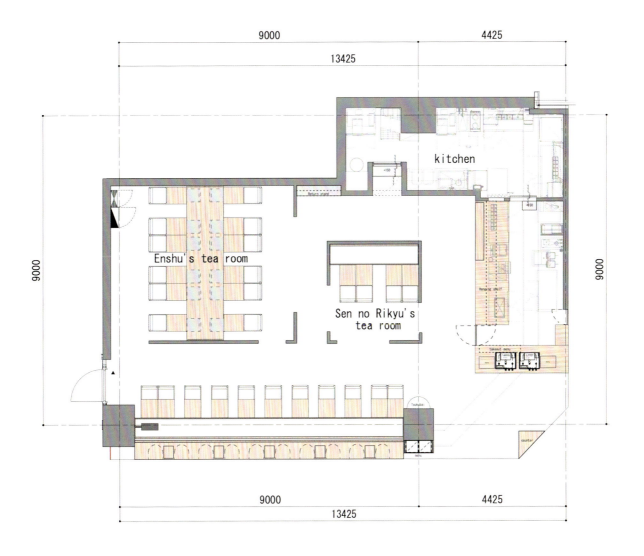

049

Shang Thai

Design Company
WUJE Design

Project Designers
WUJE Design team

Project Location
China

Site Area
400 m²

The design of this case was inspired by a painting by the designer's daughter, 'By the Sea'. In the picture, the four sunken twilights are set against the starry river under the sea, there are shell-like tents and the bright sea of sand seems to be on fire, which moves the viewer. The designer loves this image of a child's pure nature, believing it to be the beauty of people's original nature and the simple joy of a child, and isn't this the essence of life that people seek?

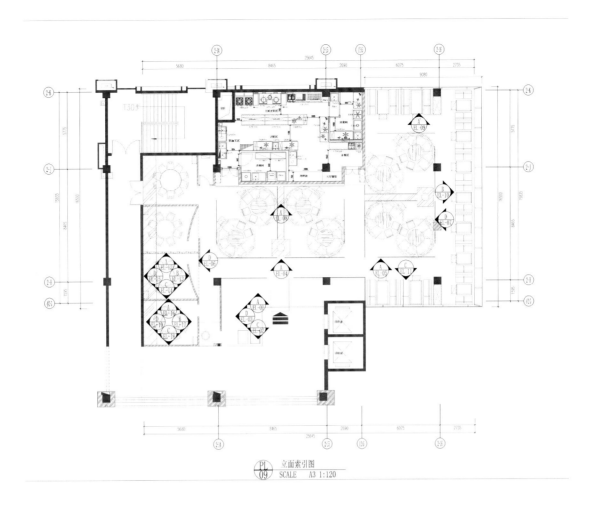

立面索引图 SCALE A3 1:120

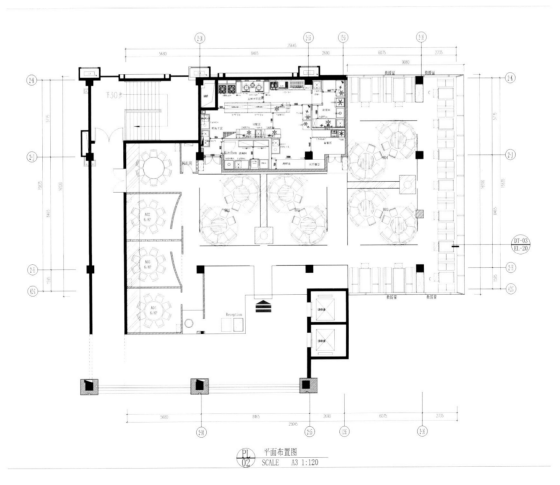

平面布置图 SCALE A3 1:120

055

HEYTEA LAB at the MixC Xiamen

Design Company
MOC DESIGN OFFICE

Project Designers
Liang Ningsen, Wu Xiuwei

Project Location
Fujian, China

Site Area
460 m^2

Based on a two-storey open-plan structure, the designer has created a bottom-up sloping structure that takes into account the various possibilities of urban living and socialising.

In the original building space, all the pipes were set on one side and there was a height difference in the space. In order to match the site conditions and maximise the interior space, the designers designed the ceiling and walls at a slight slope. This creative solution effectively resolves the limitations of the site and artistically realises the design values.

The geometric divisions and combinations of forms in the neighbourhood provide a variety of experiences that meet diverse spatial needs and are in keeping with the original spirit of HEYTEA. Structure, materials, architecture and environment are harmoniously integrated as a whole and as an urban gathering place to serve the public.

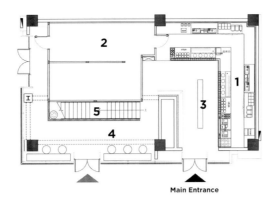

1F

1 Counter
2 Kitchen
3 Drinking Stand
4 Fast Seating
5 Stairs
6 Tea Geek Lab
7 Product Display
8 H-Gift Area
9 Art Area
10 High Seating
11 Comfort Seating
12 Washroom

Main Entrance

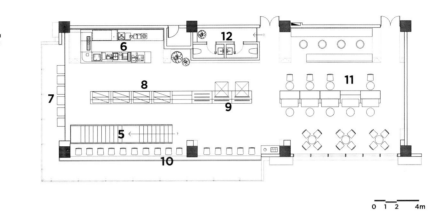

2F

0 1 2 4m

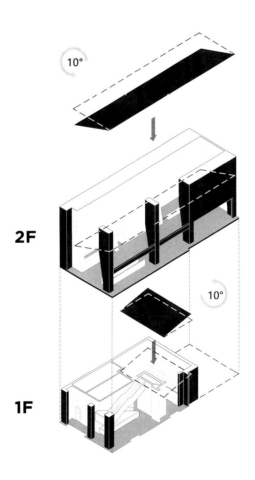

2F

1F

The Unity of Zen and Martial Arts

Design Company
UND Design Studio

Project Designers
Ma Yingkang, Ma Yanhao, Zhang Mingtong, Huang Shubin, Wang Runwei

Project Location
Guangdong, China

Site Area
175 m²

The design is located in Foshan, the hometown of martial arts, where was once famous for Wing Chun. Designers try to integrate modern aesthetics with brand culture, combining the local culture of Foshan with oriental zen in the same space to interpret the unity of zen and martial arts. The challenge lies in how to combine geographical characteristics with brand culture, satisfying modern young people to enjoy tea while evoking the perception of traditional culture. How to express traditional cultural symbols in modern times is also the theme of the exploration.

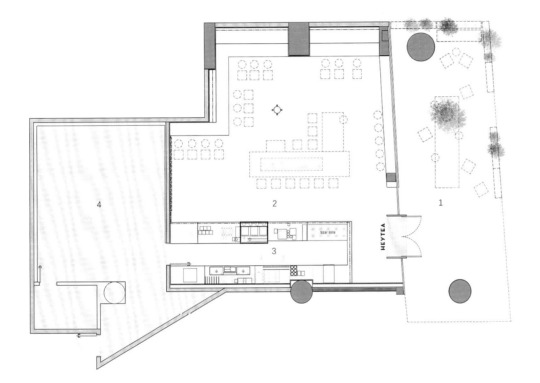

PLAN

1. External Pendulum region
2. Dining area
3. Water Bar area
4. Kitchen area

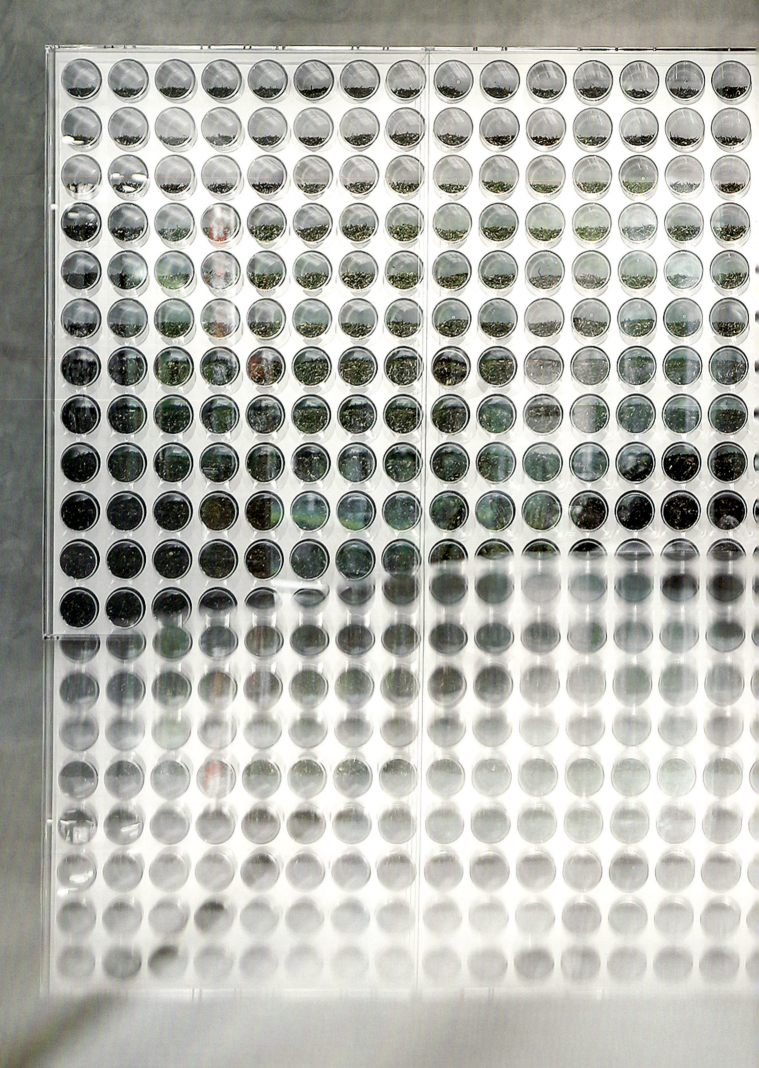

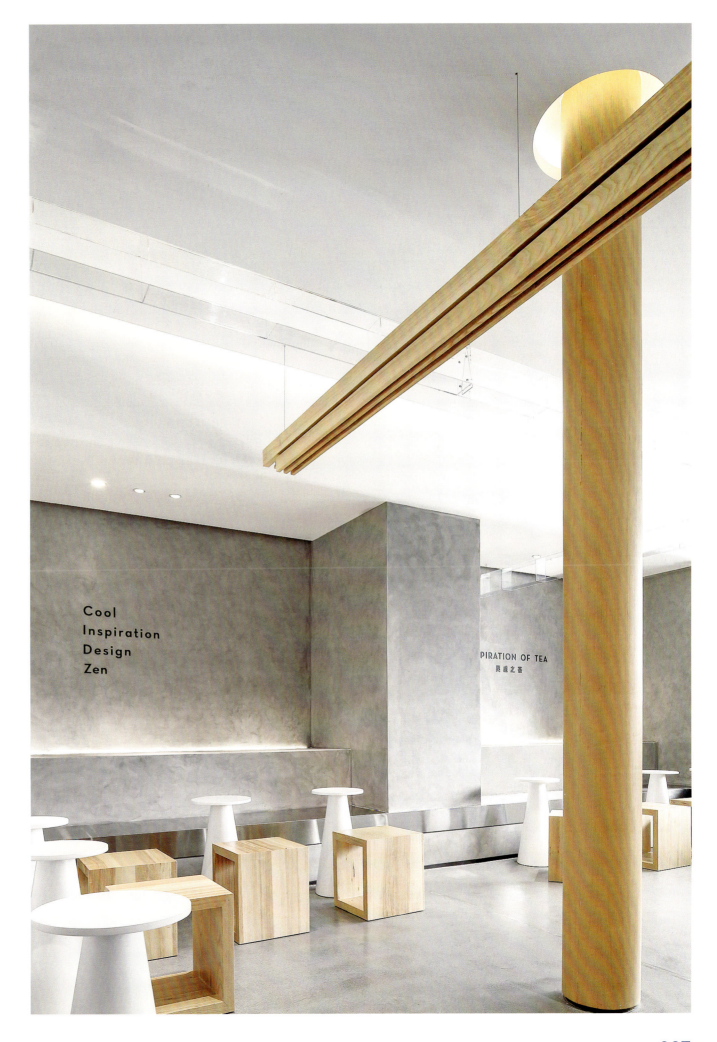

Cool
Inspiration
Design
Zen

Food Space

Honourable Mention

WU

Design Company
AD Architecture

Project Designers
Xie Peihe

Project Location
Guangdong, China

Site Area
600 m²

Located in Shantou, Guangdong, the project is positioned as a new-style private club of Teochew cuisine. It inherits the delicious Teochew cuisine while embodying a business idea and a spatial environment that keep up with the modernity.

The designer drew on geometrical lines and shapes to form the space form, which overturns the traditional design and style of Teochew cuisine restaurant. The design emphasizes space aesthetics and pays more attention to the ambience of space. The quiet light controls the main ambience of the overall space, making customers fully immersed in the environment, in which they can have a unique and illusory experience.

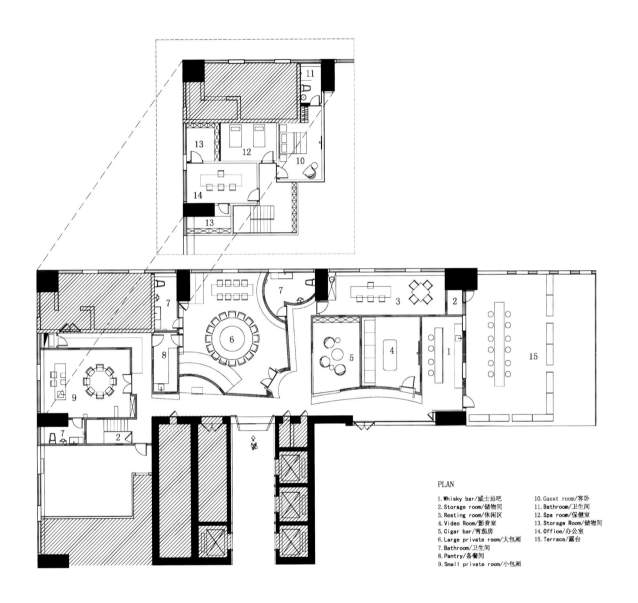

PLAN
1. Whisky bar/威士忌吧
2. Storage room/储物间
3. Resting room/休闲区
4. Video Room/影音室
5. Cigar bar/雪茄房
6. Large private room/大包厢
7. Bathroom/卫生间
8. Pantry/备餐间
9. Small private room/小包厢
10. Guest room/客卧
11. Bathroom/卫生间
12. Spa room/保健室
13. Storage Room/储物间
14. Office/办公室
15. Terrace/露台

071

INSTALLATION & EXHIBITION SPACE

Installation & Exhibition Space

Gold

Aranya Art Center

Design Company
Neri&Hu Design and Research Office

Project Designers
Lyndon Neri & Rossana Hu, Nellie Yang, Ellen Chen, Jerry Guo, Utsav Jain, Josh Murphy, Gianpaolo Taglietti, Zoe Gao, Susana Sanglas, Brian Lo, Lili Cheng

Project Location
Hebei, China

Site Area
1500 m²

The design process for the Aranya Art Center has seen the designers explore the concept of art space and public space. Aranya is organised as a community to enhance people's spiritual life, in harmony with the environment. The design solution is therefore to create both a public space and an exhibition space for the residents.

The designers drew inspiration from the seasonal changes of the nearby ocean, with the idea of a comprehensive display of the natural wonders of water at the heart of the design. The scheme is a simple circular geometry carved out of the centre of the building, with a stepped amphitheatre style design below. The void space in between is a water feature when filled with water, and a performance area and space for relaxation and gathering when emptied of water. At night, the open design allows light to penetrate and the building appears as a jewel in the waterfront community.

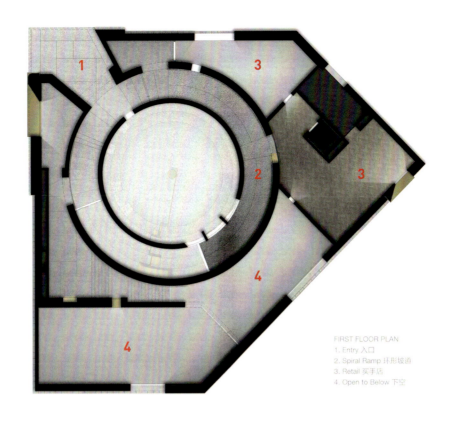

FIRST FLOOR PLAN
1. Entry 入口
2. Spiral Ramp 环形坡道
3. Retail 买手店
4. Open to Below 下空

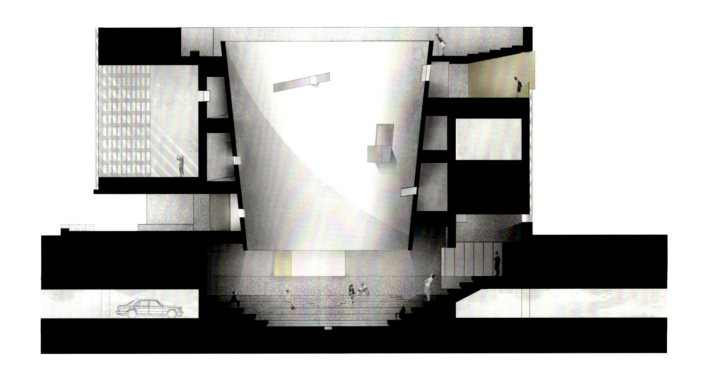

079

Installation & Exhibition Space

Silver

UTTER SPACE

Design Company
CUN Design

Project Designers
Shu Cui, Chuan Ma

Project Location
Beijing, China

Site Area
2,000 m²

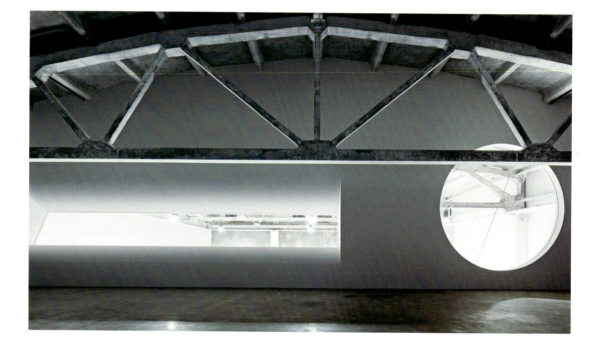

Liu Zongyuan's Beijing photography studio UTTER SPACE is located in a warehouse in a 1960s old building in Beijing. The original purpose of the space was also a film studio. After the space design renovation, designer restored the original appearance of the old building, revealing its historical traces and time beauty. It changed the nature of the space from purely serving the needs of photography work to a compound space integrating work, art gallery and social activities. The main materials are marble, latex paint, wood veneer, iron plate, cement artesian equality.

First Floor Plan Image

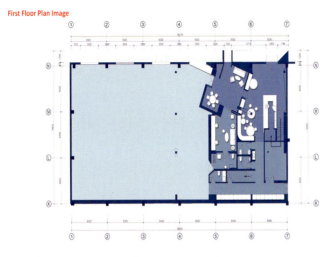

Second Floor Plan Image

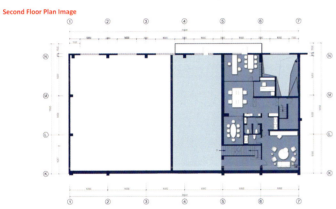

Third Floor Plan Image

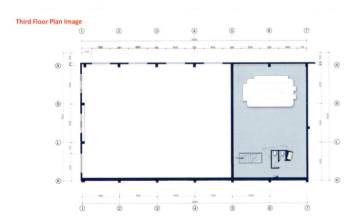

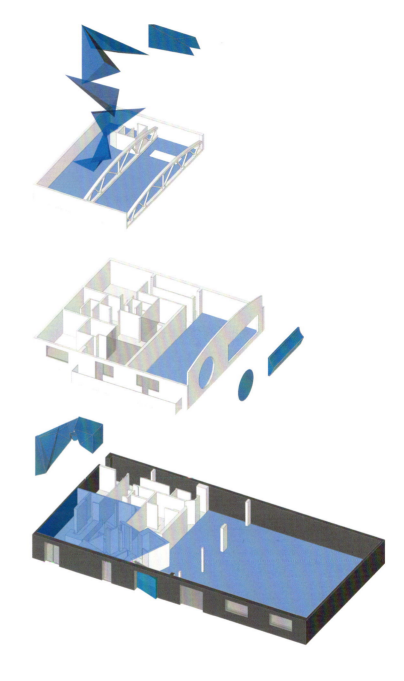

087

Yingliang Stone Natural History Museum

Design Company
Atelier Alter Architects

Project Designers
Yingfan Zhang, Xiaojun Bu, Zhenwei Li, Jiahe Zhang, Lairong Zheng, Bo Huang, Leilei Ma

Project Location
Fujian, China

Site Area
2,600 m²

The project sites at the office headquarter of a stone manufacturer in Xiamen. The project transforms the principal of stone dissection into a spatial division mechanism, to cut the cubical space accordingly. Besides that, the geometric logic of crystal is also introduced as a way to tight the irregular spatial parts together. The orthogonal office space is transformed into a mysterious triangulated space. As the heavy mass floating up, the anti-gravity space places the audience in an unknown space seemly coming straight from a Sci-fi film.

The architectural element of the wall is used throughout the project to continue the consistency and authenticity of the project. The structure is simple and clear: a lightweight frame and plasterboard are used for the substructure, and a double concrete slab is used for the surfaces of the interior spaces, creating a sense of calm and coolness in the cavern where the fossils are stored.

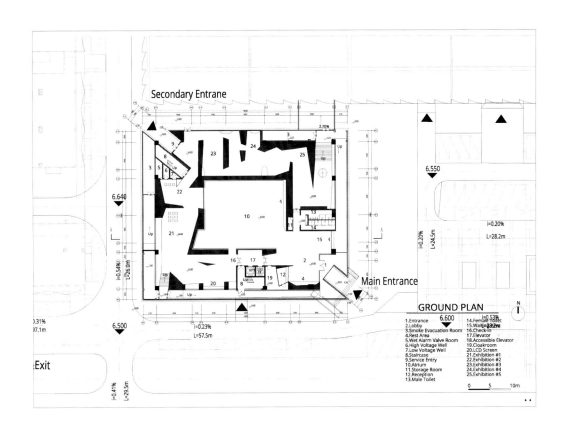
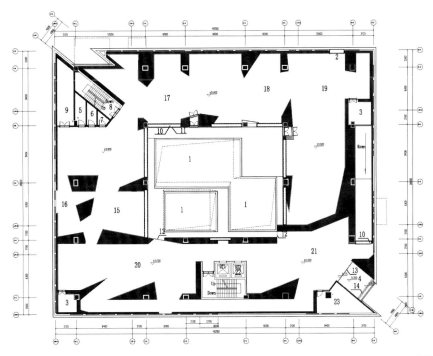

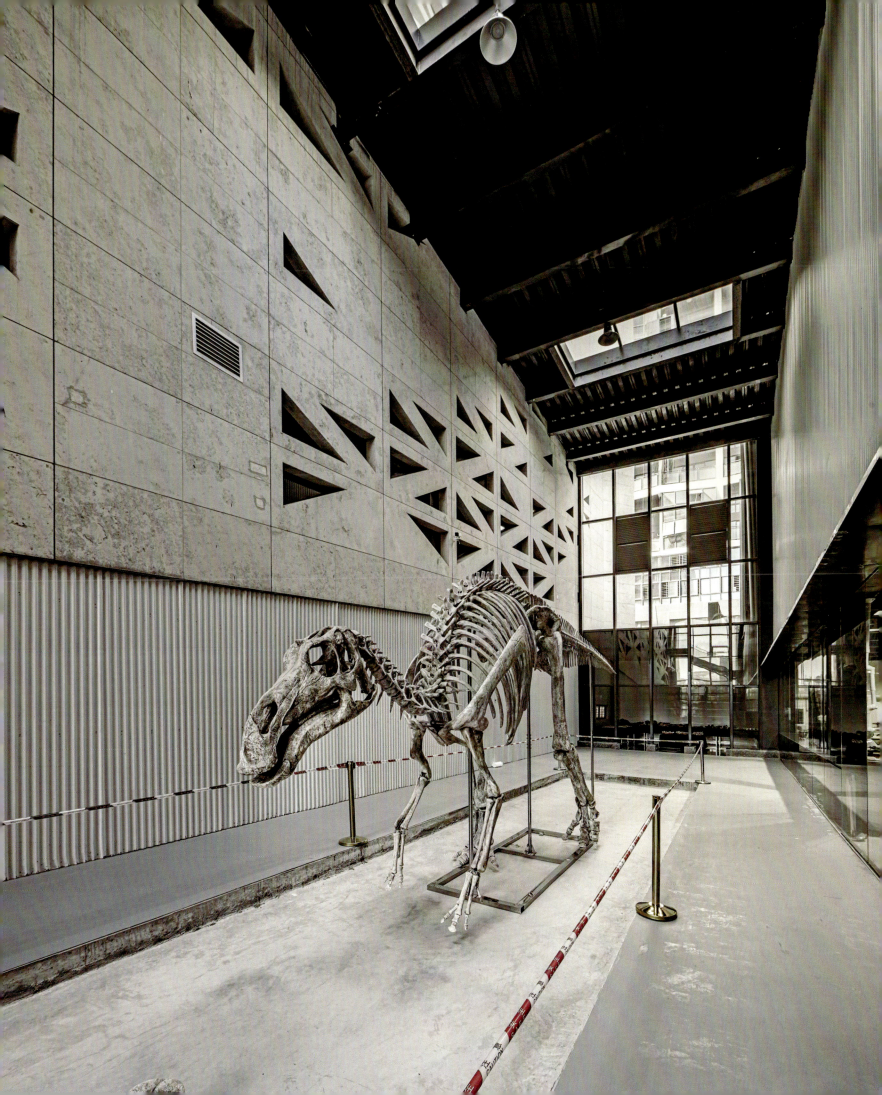

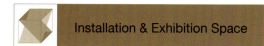

Newton and Moon

Design Company
DOMANI Architectural Concepts

Project Designers
Ann Yu

Project Location
Guangdong, China

Site Area
2,000 m²

The sales center of Faithland Group in Shenzhen has the combined functions of operation, sales negotiation and free reading of citizens. The space will be converted into a public children's activity center in 5 years. Therefore, the function of space needs to have strong variability and orientation that is "precise and vague". The idea of unknown and freedom is the concept of creation, which is the thread through the project in different time lines, targeted at different people, and a perpetual clue in different places. The decentralized free moving line is the construction method of the space.

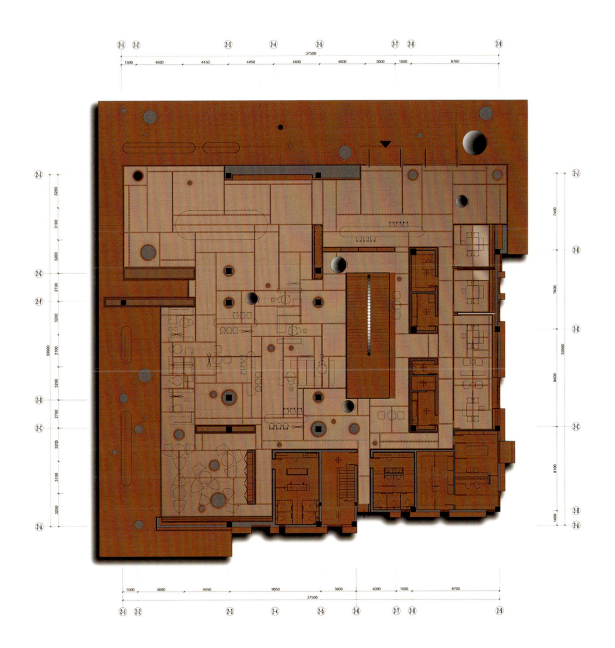

Artizon Museum

Design Company
TONERICO:INC.

Project Designers
Hiroshi Yoneya, Ken Kimizuka

Project Location
Tokyo, Japan

Site Area
261.4 m²

The project is designed to express "nature of empty and misalignment" in this space, which seems purposeless, you see the void and sense the misalignments.

Designers use the principle of white space in painting, so that the blank space is still in contact with the perception of other elements, which will stimulate visitors' imagination.

In addition to utilizing primitive methods of constructing the space, this work attempts to see its totality through pushing chains of seemingly random elements, thus achieving a natural state through misalignments.

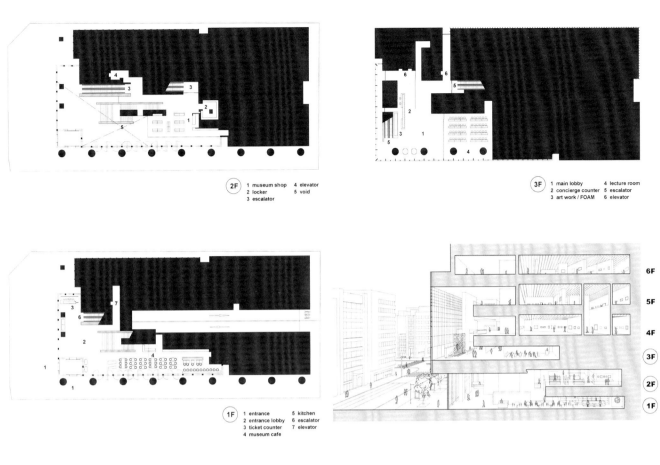

2F
1 museum shop   4 elevator
2 locker   5 void
3 escalator

3F
1 main lobby   4 lecture room
2 concierge counter 5 escalator
3 art work / FOAM   6 elevator

1F
1 entrance   5 kitchen
2 entrance lobby 6 escalator
3 ticket counter 7 elevator
4 museum cafe

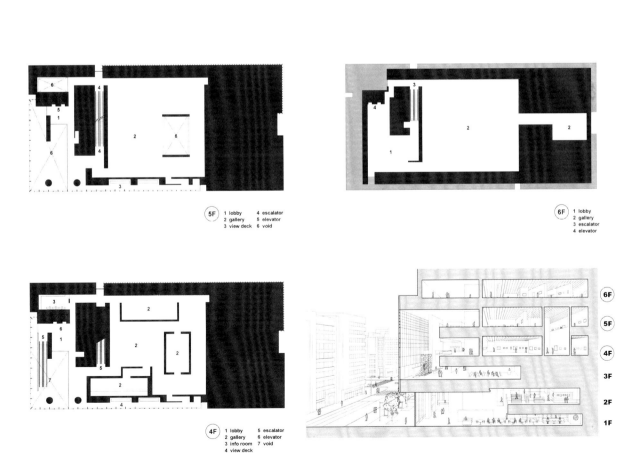

5F
1 lobby   4 escalator
2 gallery   5 elevator
3 view deck 6 void

6F
1 lobby
2 gallery
3 escalator
4 elevator

4F
1 lobby   5 escalator
2 gallery   6 elevator
3 info room 7 void
4 view deck

103

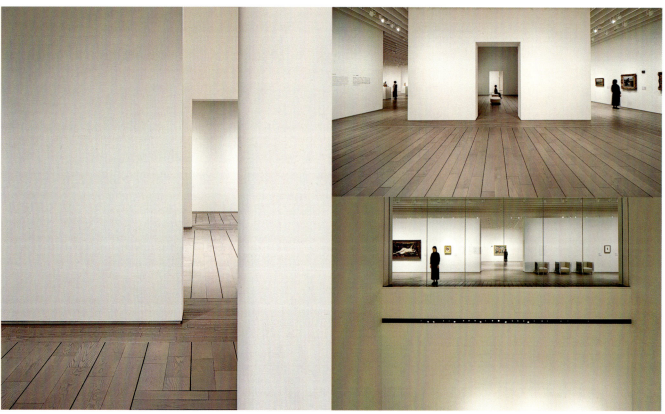

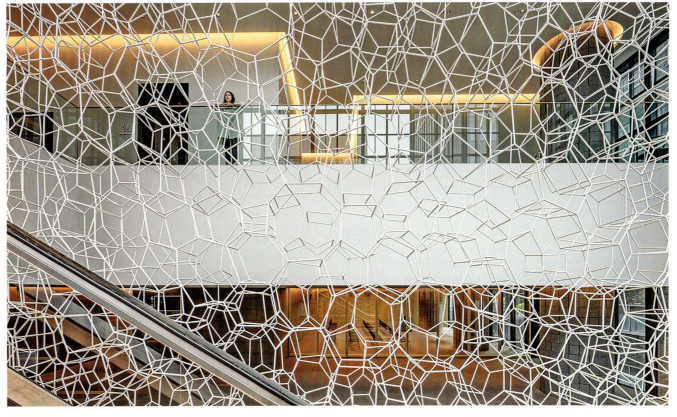

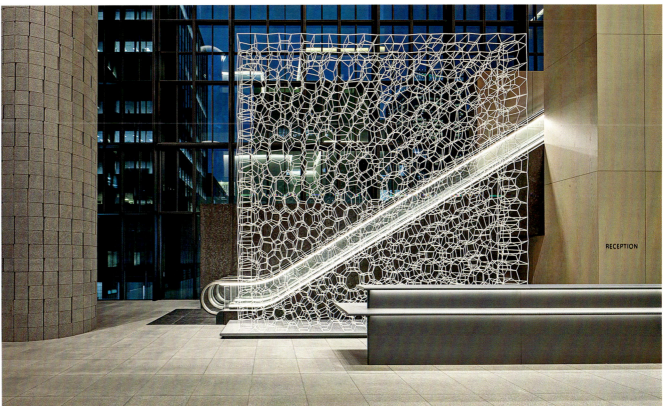

LEISURE & ENTERTAINMENT SPACE

Exhibition of Frozen Time

Design Company
Waterfrom Design Co., Ltd.

Project Designers
Li Zhixiang, Guo Ruiwen, Lin Tingyu, Dai Zuoying

Project Location
Beijing, China

Site Area
280 m²

The clinic attempts to use cosmetic SPA and technological atmosphere to twist the impression of traditional Chinese medicine. This place enables people to jointly shape the contemporary five-senses culture through space, diet, and SPA, as well as experience the ancient internal and external health cultivation of traditional medicine. Designer enable visitors to experience the tenderness in an environment rich in technological and medical principles by receiving the diagnosis and treatment of traditional medicine or SPA care. Such tenderness comes from the sense of slowness of detachment from time and space, refinement, and endless aftertaste from art.

111

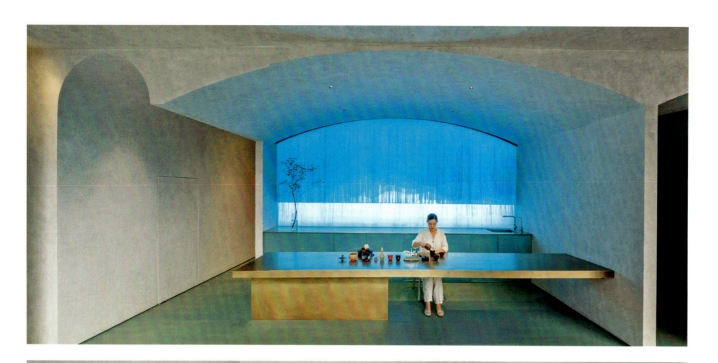

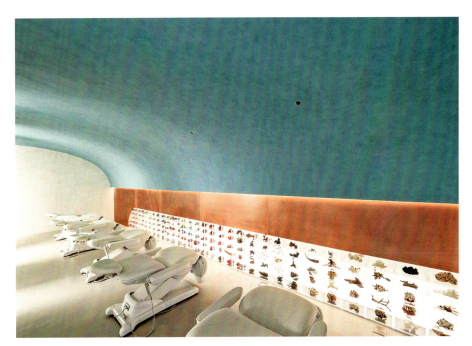

113

Xi'an Changjiang Insun Cinema

Design Company
One Plus Partnership Limited

Project Designers
Ajax Law, Virginia Lung

Project Location
Shaanxi, China

Site Area
4,154 m²

The project takes "negative film" as the design theme, which is presented in the whole cinema space. It is intended to relive the wonderful memories of the era of film in the time when full use of digital technology. This concept is particularly reflected in the color design, which presents strong color contrast like negative film.

On the other hand, the design combines the concept of family-friendly and fully functional playground, welcoming children and adults to interact and play in the space before and after the film is shown.

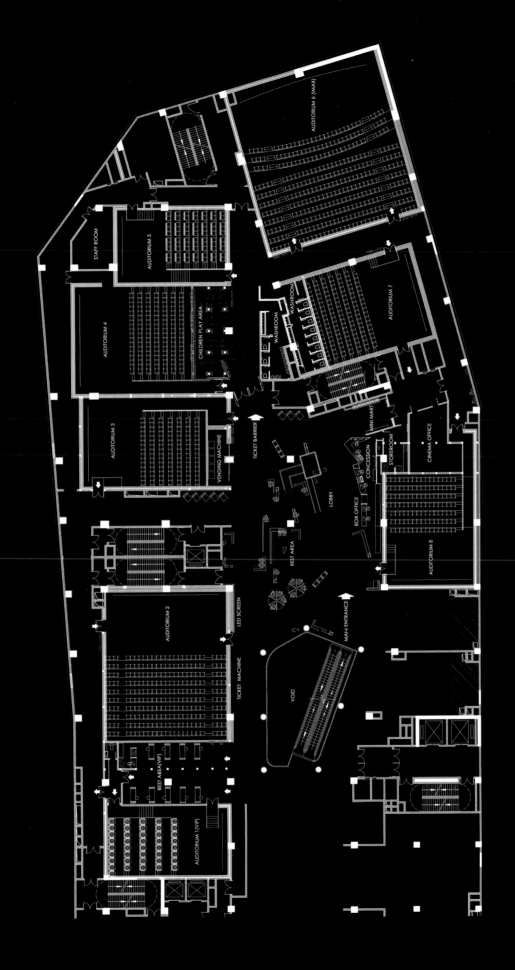

Changsha Insun International Cinema

Design Company
One Plus Partnership Limited

Project Designers
Ajax Law, Virginia Lung

Project Location
Hunan, China

Site Area
5,980 m²

This project takes the traditional megaphone as the theme, because the film director holds the megaphone in hand to dispatch and arrange the lighting man, photographer and actor on site, and the megaphone has also become the symbol of the film director. The designer is inspired by megaphone shape, splits the traditional megaphone mouth shape and then recreates, integrated into the lobby of the entire theater, the bathroom, the space, and the modelling of seat, lamps also has the same trick. The design is both combined with the overall space and seizes the presentation of the details.

Due to the low budget of the project, grey paint was used to render the entire walls and ceiling, giving the space a strong aesthetic effect as if it had been sculpted in stone. In addition to gray, bright orange was also chosen to decorate the space, symbolizing the Orange Continent of Changsha.

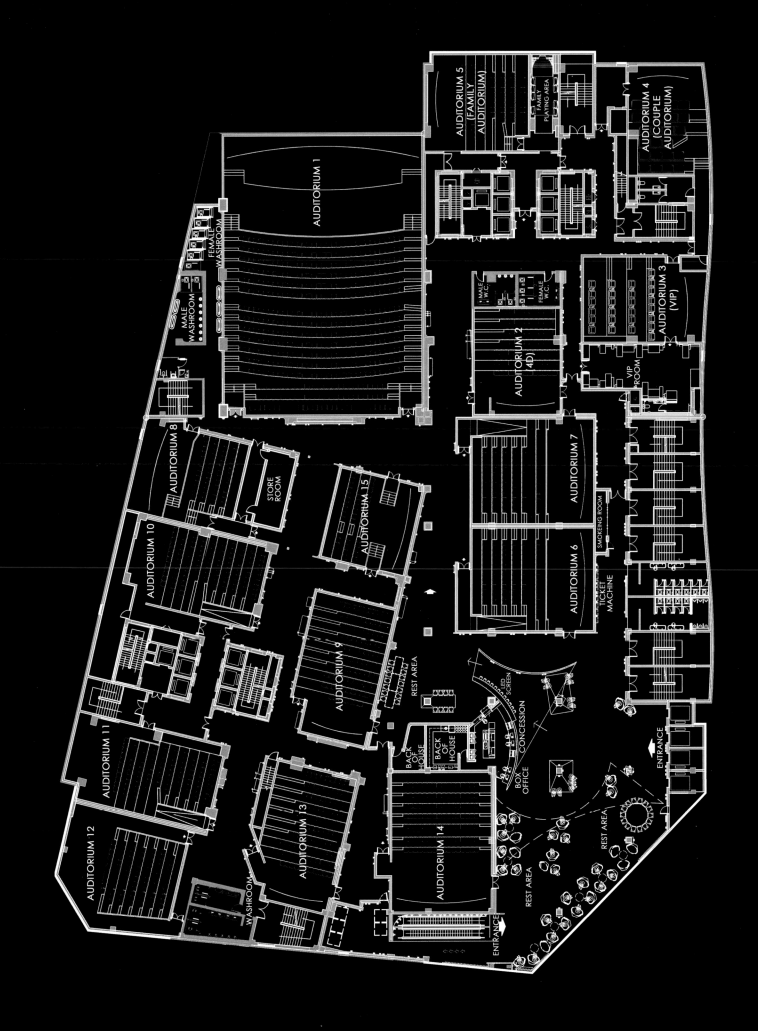

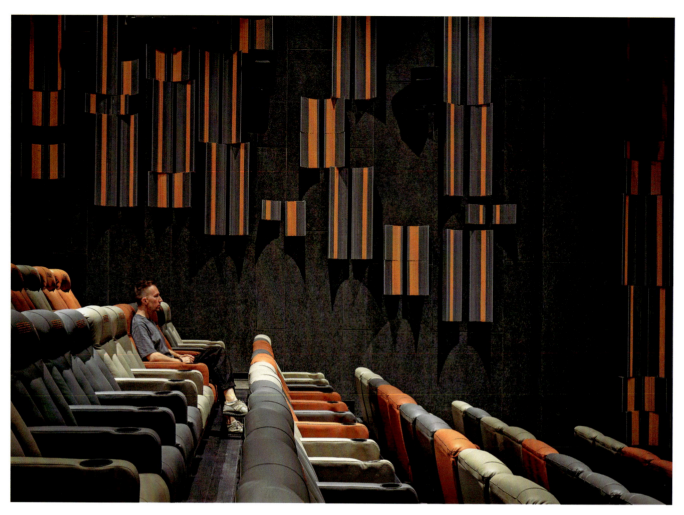
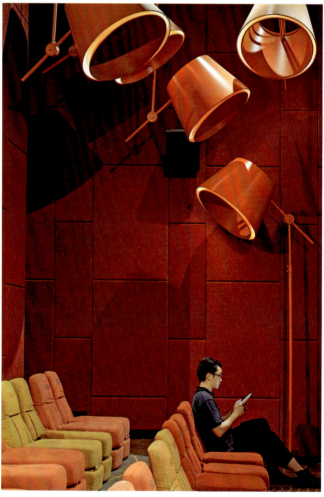

Leisure & Entertainment Space

Honourable Mention

Sanshui Cultural Centre

Design Company
Basic Design

Project Designers
Liang Zhide, Li Wanli, Chang Forever, Ye Shujuan

Project Location
Guangdong, China

Site Area
5,000 m²

The lotus in the wind sways gracefully and sends off pleasant fragrance. Sanshui Cultural Centre is located in Hexiang Lake, the core area of Sanshui New Town, Foshan City. As a new cultural landmark of Sanshui District, its architectural appearance and interior design are of high standards.

The theatre is designed with a total of 1,200 seats, equipped with advanced domestic audio machinery and other equipment. Architectural acoustics and indoor acoustics echo each other, by which a theatre space for audio-visual feasts is created.

The indoor wall is of double curved surface. Pieces of natural and plain wood veneer constitute pieces of angular visual sections. The layered space is of wood and red hue, and the artistic sound transmit in the fluctuating space, which is quite attractive.

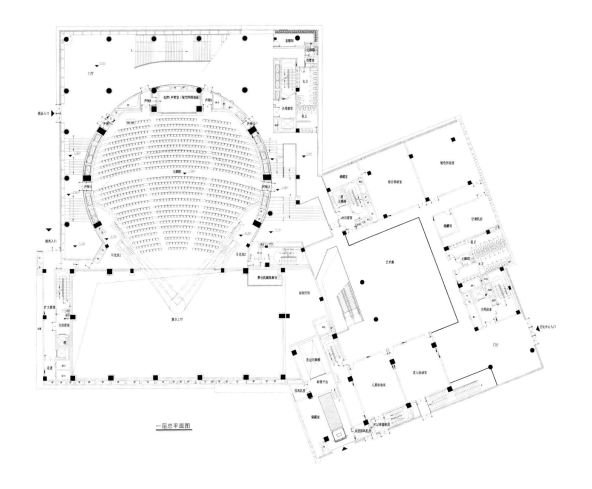

一层总平面图

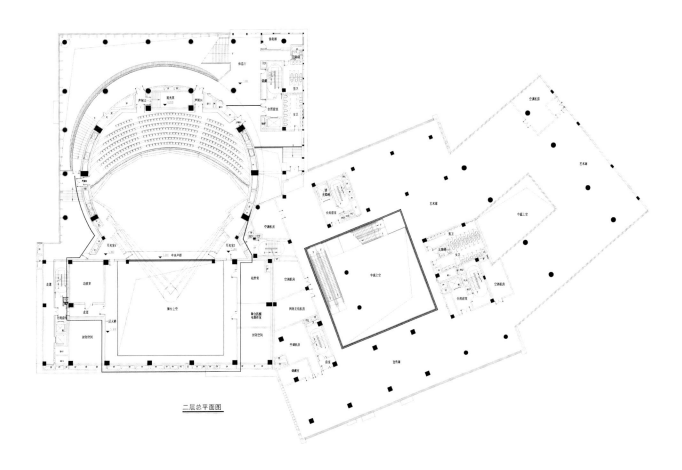

二层总平面图

Leisure & Entertainment Space

Honourable Mention

TaiOursea SPA Shop

Design Company
RoarcRenew

Project Designers
Bai Zhenqi, Lin Yan, Xue Leqian, Lu Huiqin, Wu Yejing, Yang Junyi, Gu Qian

Project Location
Jiangsu, China

Site Area
450 m²

This project is a Thai spa experience located in the old city of Nanjing, China. The primary consideration in the design was how to express Thai elements without creating an abrupt and incongruous feeling in such an old Chinese city, and to combine and express the two cultures organically. As a result, the designers have refined and used cultural symbols such as 'red bricks' and 'lanterns' to express the similarities and differences between the two cultures of Nanjing, China and Northern Thailand.

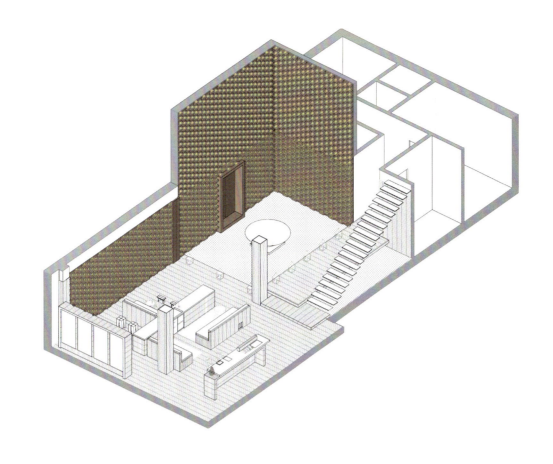

1 接待
2 换鞋
3 洽谈
4 沐足
5 卫生间
6 庭院
7 精油SPA
8 后勤

1 古风SPA
2 精油SPA
3 卫生间
4 后勤

1F PLAN　　　　2F PLAN

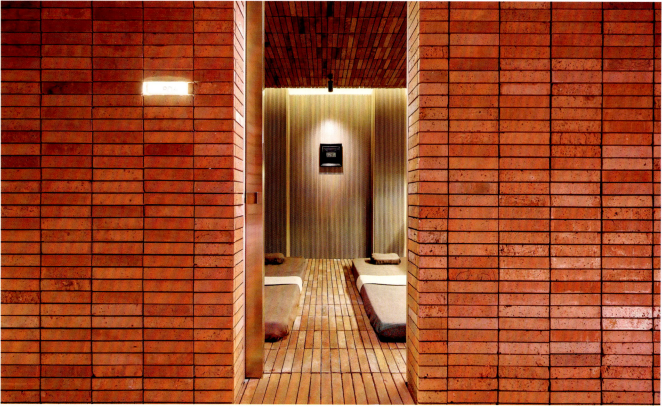

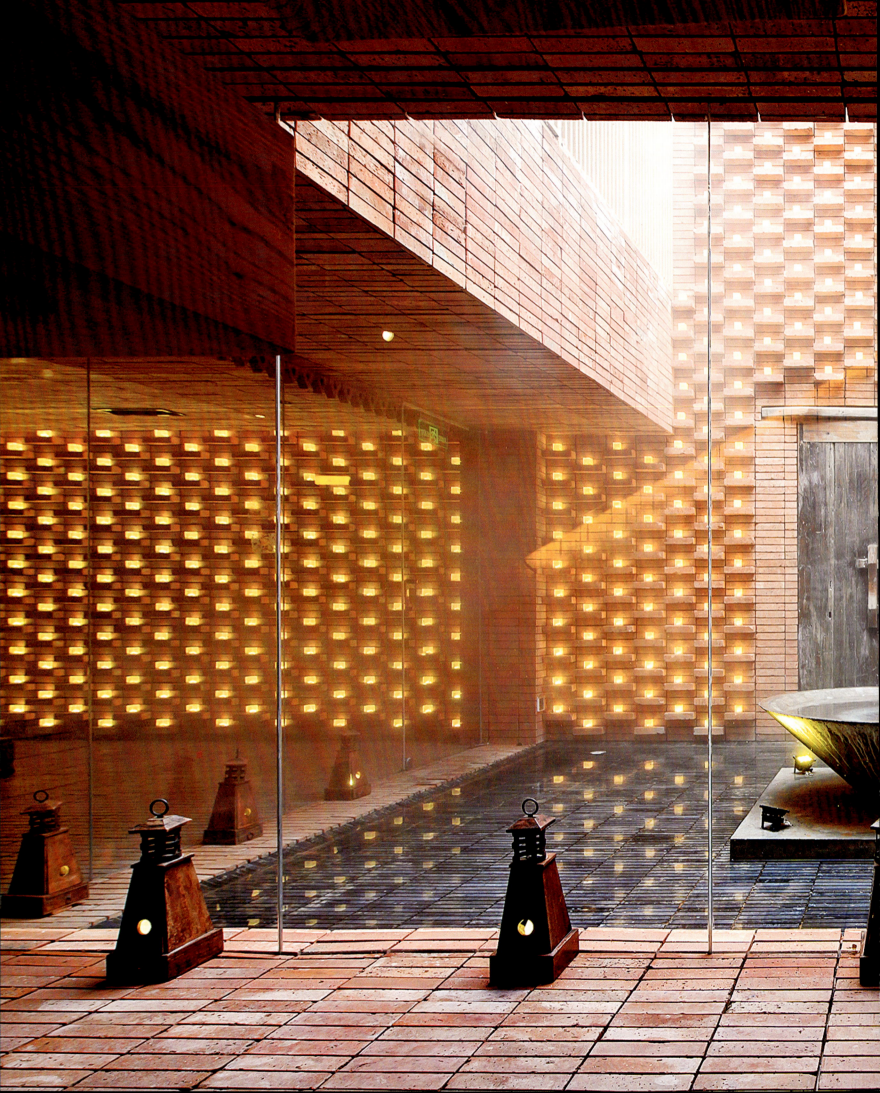

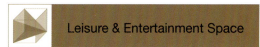

Leisure & Entertainment Space

Honourable Mention

Backstage Glory

Design Company
One Plus Partnership Limited

Project Designers
Ajax Law, Virginia Lung

Project Location
Hubei, China

Site Area
2,950 m²

At the very beginning of the film production, the producers, directors and screenwriters all gathered around the desk to brainstorm story ideas and main characters. After that, the writer would lean on the sofa in front of the workbench, and rush towards the desk to write down any new ideas on the documents whenever he suddenly thinks of a wonderful plot. Finally, the artist would draw the storyboard for filming preparation. The audience would not have the chance to see this series of behind-the-scenes work, but these are the reasons why classical films are being made. Films are a combination of collective wisdom and creativity for all behind-the-scenes creators, and impact thousands of people worldwide.

The project's design was inspired by the process of film creation and presented the audience with this interactive behind-the-scenes working space.

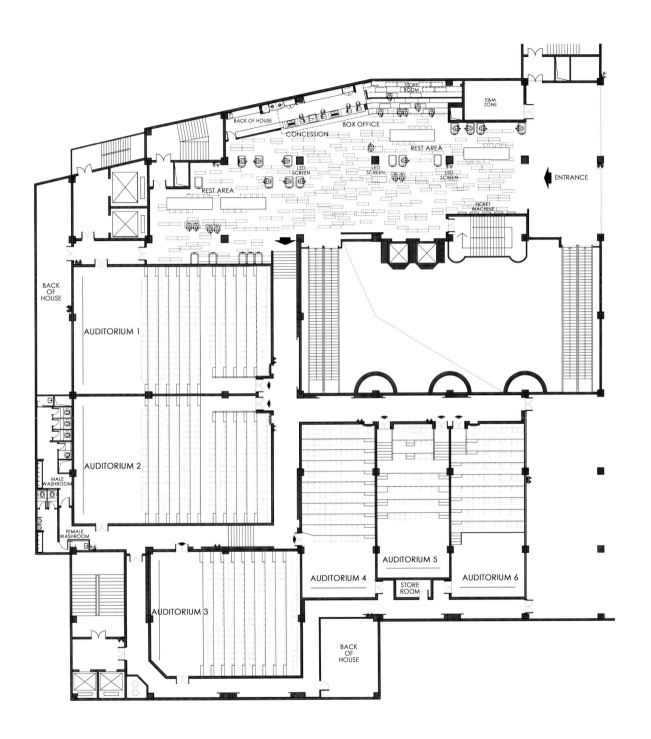

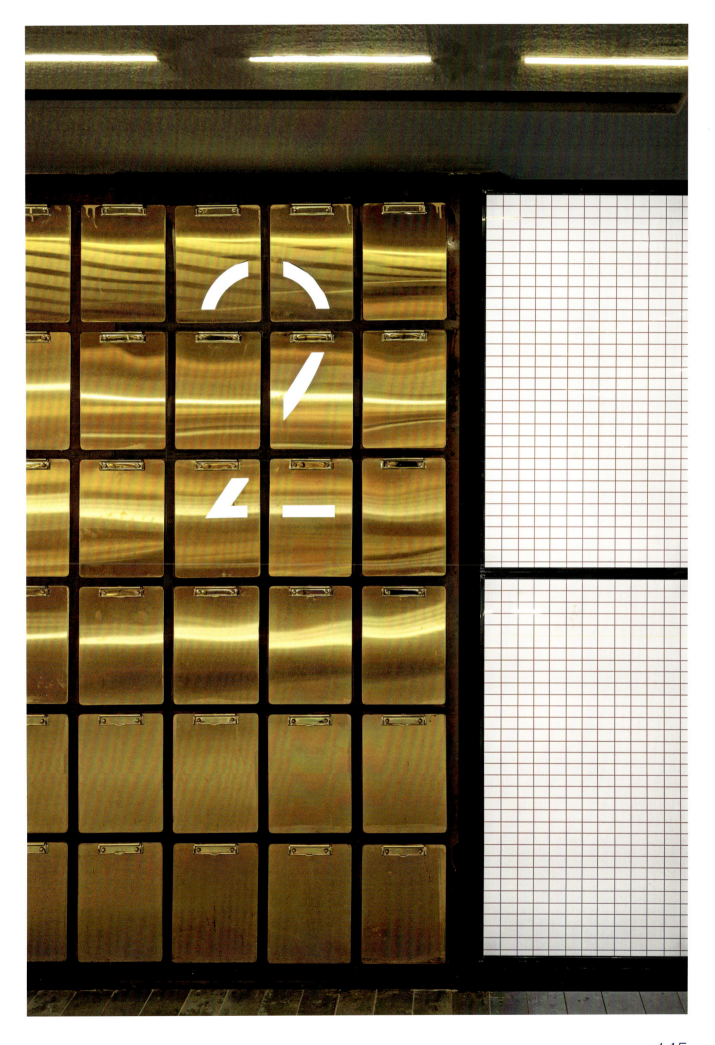

INSTITUTIONAL SPACE

Enjoy the Time

Design Company
C&C Design Co.,Ltd.

Project Designers
Peng Zheng, Lian Yuanchao, Liang Jingshan

Project Location
China

Site Area
1,073 m²

The design creatively integrates the public welfare city reading center and the sales office, combining the arc-shaped flow lines of the building and the dual drainage entrances inside and outside the mall, taking into account the book consumption traffic flow and the house purchase experience traffic flow to form functional zones and mutual diversion. Book walls and ladders structure the integrity and interactivity of the space. The reading area is relatively independent and retains pure reading experience for customers. The entire design abandons strong expression style and completes the connection between the space and individual through the whole scene.

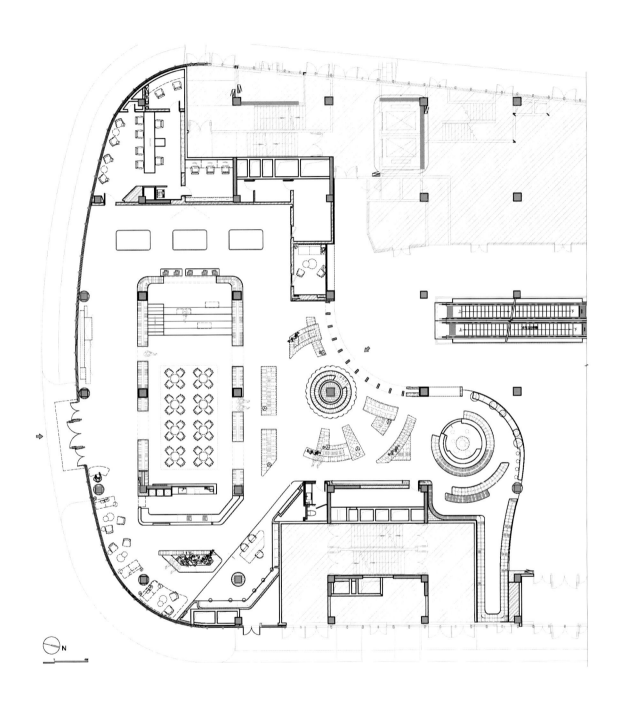

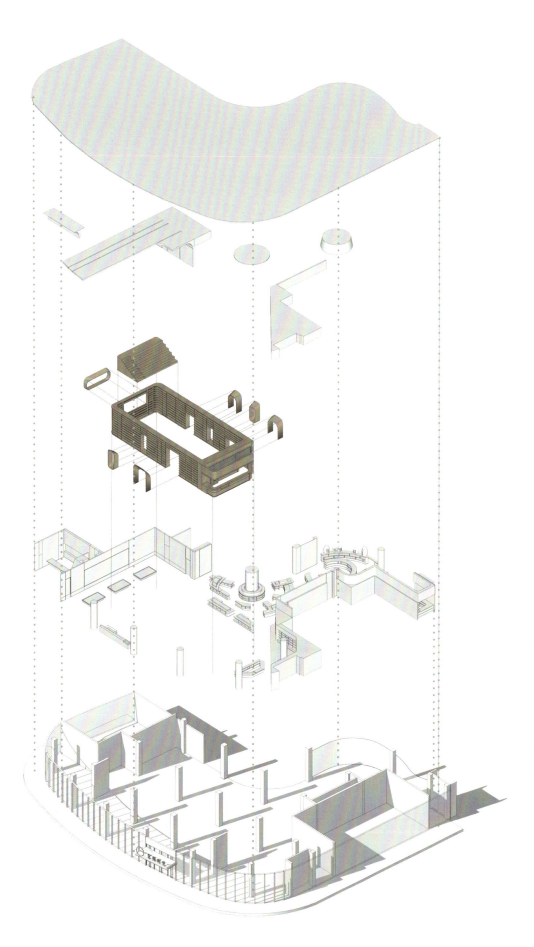

Institutional Space

Silver

Reading Under the Lake

Design Company
Waterfrom Design Co., Ltd.

Project Designers
Li Zhixiang, Ge Zhuwei, Lin Qiwei, Huang Yucheng, Chen Youru

Project Location
Fujian, China

Site Area
750 m²

The design focuses on satisfying the application scene of the community in the future, while connecting the emotional memory of Xiamen people, with trees and tea as the core design elements. In the past, an old tree always acted as the core of the gathering among the villagers, who exchanged daily information and built relationships. It is a habit and a collective memory to gather under the old tree. Tea is the tradition and essence of the traditional Xiamen culture. Drinking tea is a gesture of freeing and calming our mind.

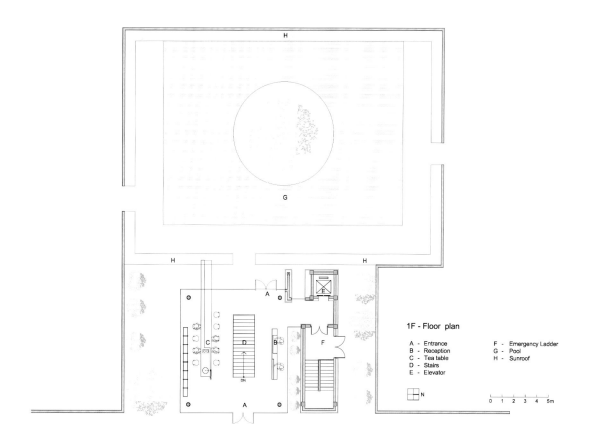
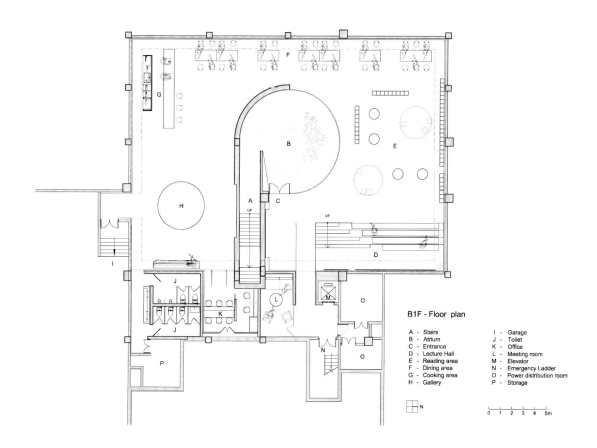

Thetford Kindergarden

Design Company
HOUPAL Interior Design

Project Designers
Jiang Bo

Project Location
Hunan, China

Site Area
1,500 m²

The 'poised' circle implies the dynamics of the space, and the blunt curves are condensed under this implicit dynamic. Static curves run through each space, interpreting the invisible inner rhythm and the life and vitality of the space. As the sunlight pours into the ground, the interior appears to be a meditation of endless mountains, embracing warmth and calm. The design incorporates an emotional attachment to the natural environment into the space, constructing forms that give soul and tension.

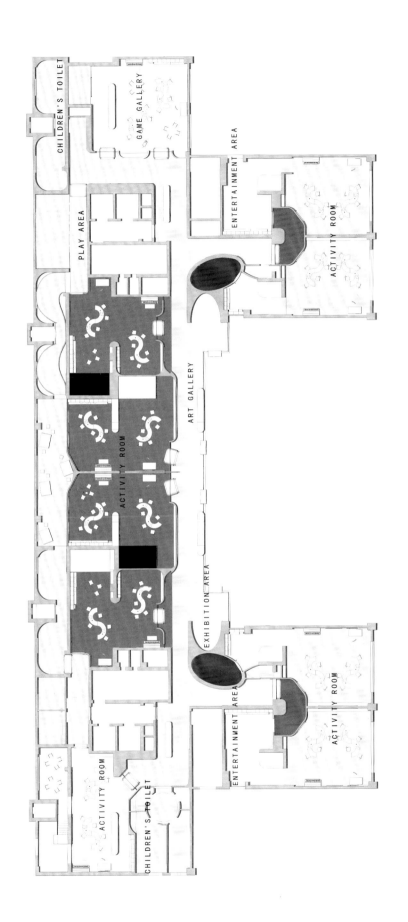

Institutional Space

Bronze

WuliEpoch Culture Centre

Design Company
Atelier Alter Architects

Project Designers
Yingfan Zhang, Xiaojun Bu, Ping Jiang, Wei Huang, Zhenwei Li, Ran Yan, Lairong Zheng, Jue Wang, Leilei Ma, Bo Huang, Chuan Qin, Lianhua Liu, Chunyu Cao, Jiang Wu, Weicong Lin

Project Location
Beijing, China

Site Area
2,880 m²

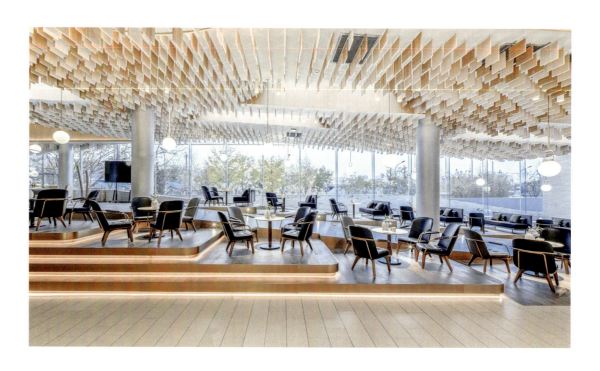

WuliEpoch Culture Centre is located near Xishan on Beijing's fifth ring road and is a mixed-use complex that combines a showcase centre and a community centre. The project attempts to create an integrated triptych of architecture, landscape and interior design. The project is surrounded by the magnificent West Hill, taking in the view of the West Hill to immerse oneself. The distant landscape is introduced into the project in a dynamic rather than static manner, with a pathway meanders from the exterior of the building to the interior, seamlessly integrating the landscape and interior spaces The design The design shows a reverence for nature, with a circular pathway that has a religiously. The interior is also a digital depiction of nature. The iconic The iconic 'Autumn Leaves of the Western Hills' image is created from a shiny wooden laminated aluminium panel, and another image, 'Inverted Western Mountain', is created by the curved arrangement of the ceiling. The other image, 'Inverted Western Mountain', is created by the curvilinear arrangement of the ceiling.

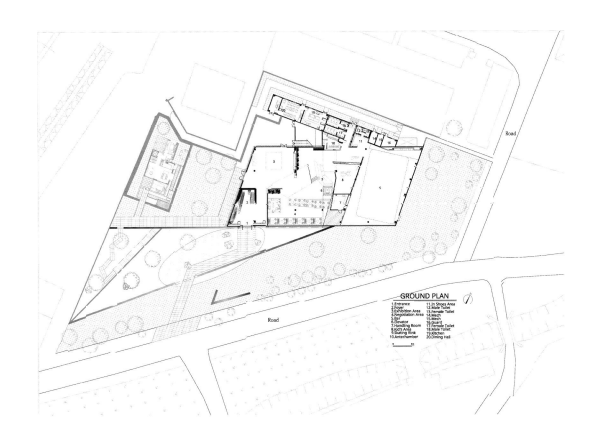
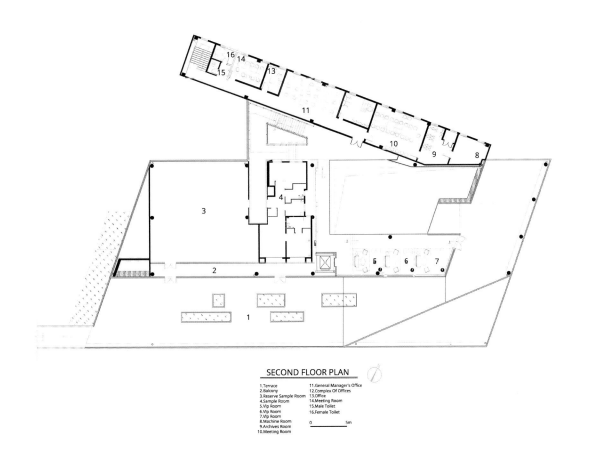

Institutional Space

Honourable Mention

Interior Renovation of the 4th Building of Tsinghua University

Design Company
Academy of Arts & Design, Tsinghua University

Project Designers
Yang Dongjiang, Yang Yu, Guan Yuanjia, Shi Shuo, Li Zhengyou, Zhang Feihe, Cao Yu, Liu Xuan

Project Location
Beijing, China

Site Area
5,000 m²

The Fourth Teaching Building (Jeanswest) of Tsinghua University has four-storey large classrooms on its west side, and five-storey public areas in the east. The mainstream of people is led by the walking stairs in the east as the major vertical traffic. The space reconstruction of the Fourth Teaching Building aims to update the equipment of the original seventy-people classrooms and add a large number of small-sized research and discussion rooms and free learning area to the existing space so that they can adapt to the current open, flexible and diversified university teaching model.

Designer hopes that the Fourth Teaching Building can become a diversified interactive place which collects class teaching, communication and research and group learning and integrate into the daily campus life space of teachers and students.

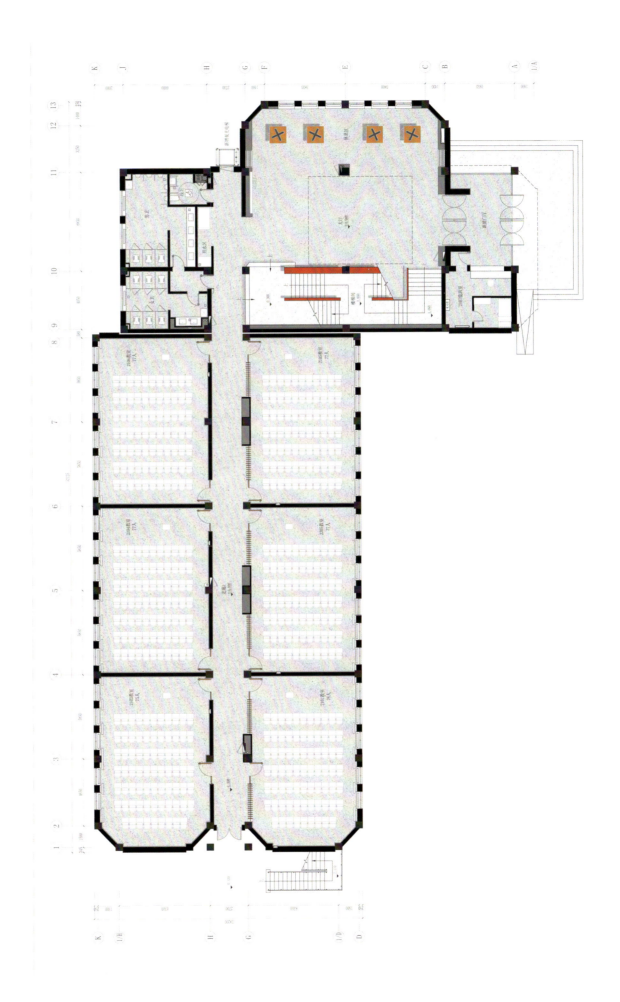

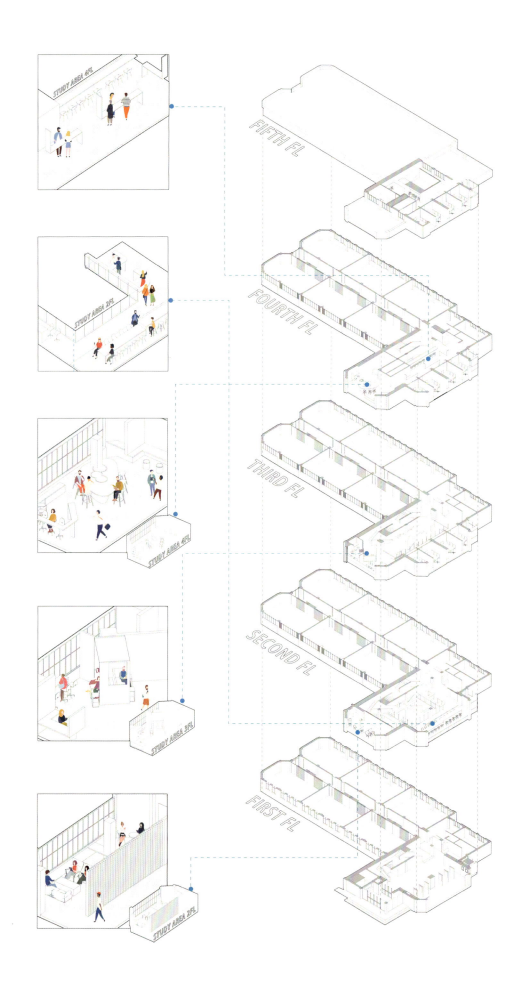

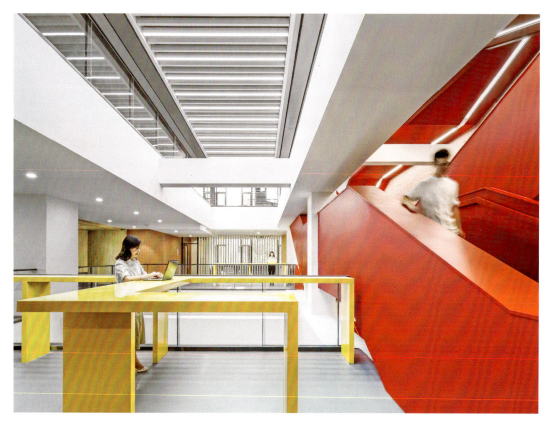
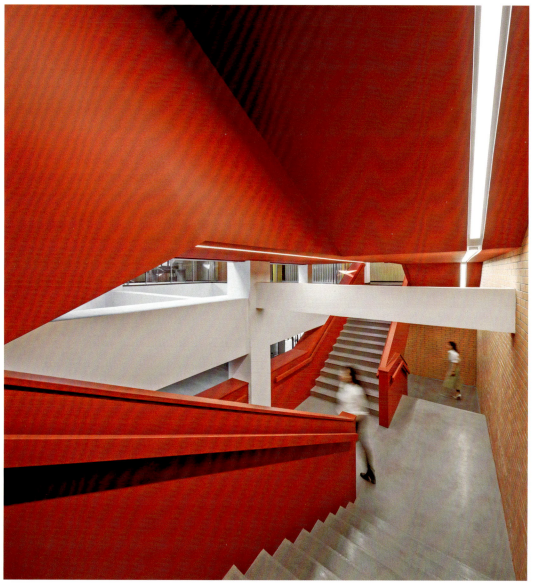

Tiny Doo Doo Pediatric Clinic

Design Company
AJAR Limited

Project Designers
Tsoi Wai Kuen, Chow Tung, Tiffany, Chan Chun Yin, Terry

Project Location
Guangdong, China

Site Area
483 m²

Tiny Doo Doo is a one-stop solution for child medical services in Panyu, and is designed to prioritise user experience, where design sensitivity is extended to every corner.

Services are split into two degrees of medical urgencies and atmospheres: G/F offers general medical and dental services, whereas 1/F is secluded and reserved for delicate patients. G/F consists of three activity zones for different ages and personalities, each with a center-piece tailor-designed to suit both adults and children: In the inward zone, children use curved tables and parents use benches; the slide for the more energetic children, is also a gathering area; the elevated play mat for babies is ergonomically designed to support mothers without straining their backs.

And segregated coves ensure privacy for individual families. Small props such as plants and crayons increase the comfort of visitors. Designated stroller parking ensures collision-free environment; smooth edges and padded corners guarantee safety; VOC-free materials warrant a toxin-free environment.

G/F | General Medical & Dental Service

1/F | Specialist & Intensive Treatment

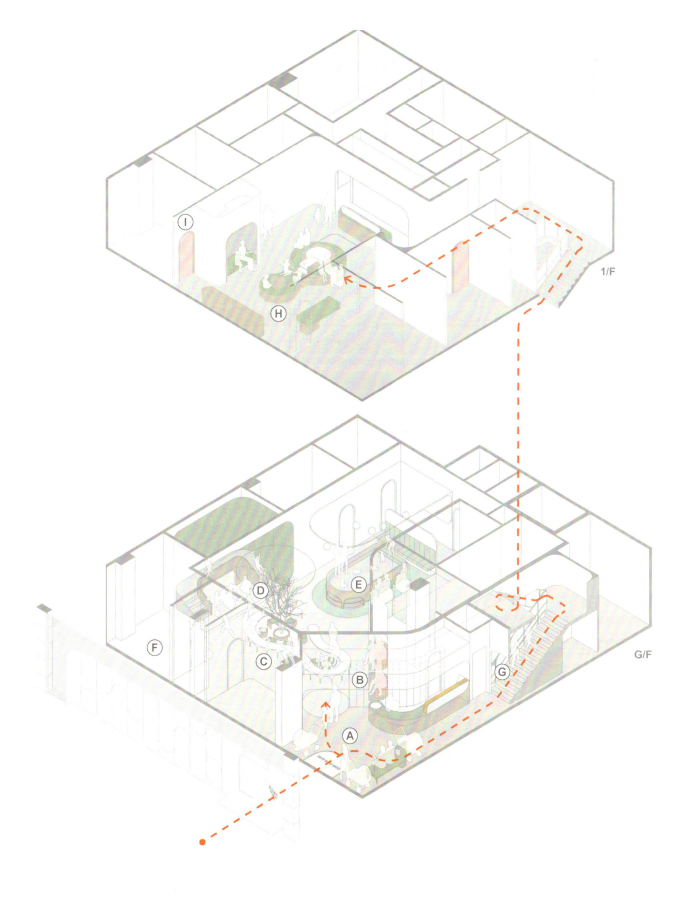

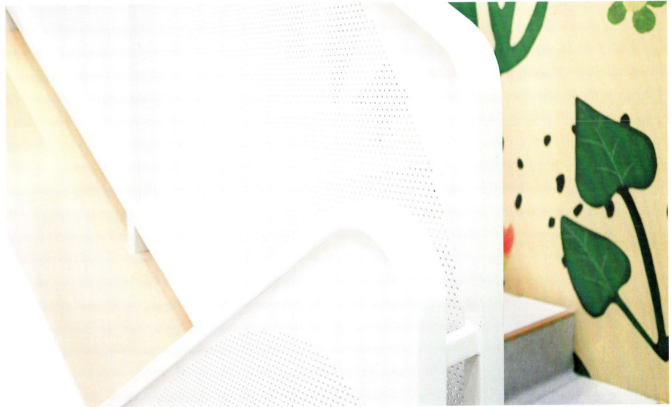

183

SHOPPING SPACE

K11 Musea

Design Company
New World Development Company Limited

Project Designers
Collaborate with AB concept, KPF, Laab & Speirs and Major

Project Location
Hong Kong, China

Site Area
30,000 m²

The project is more than just a place to shop; it also highlights culture, art and design. K11 has teamed up with 100 artists from different disciplines and cultures to revitalise the mall and make K11 Musea a cultural Silicon Valley, infusing art, architecture, design, sustainable environmental concepts and culture in all its forms into the daily lives of new consumers.

Inspired by the 'Muse by the Sea', the centrepiece of the mall is a 35-metre high atrium, known as the 'Opera House', which consists of approximately 1,800 programmable spotlights that look like a galaxy, evoking a sense of wonder and creativity in the form of galaxies and mysterious stellar bodies. curiosity and creativity. The elaborate arrangement of lights on the opera-like ceiling creates a 'creative galaxy', with a giant sphere installation acting as a focal point for the audience, further enhancing the illusion that one is looking into space.

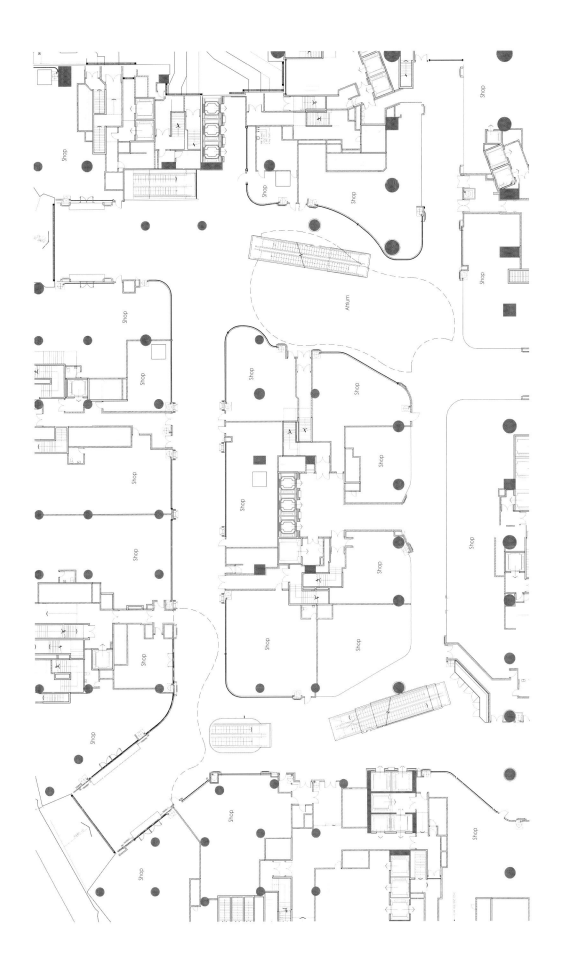

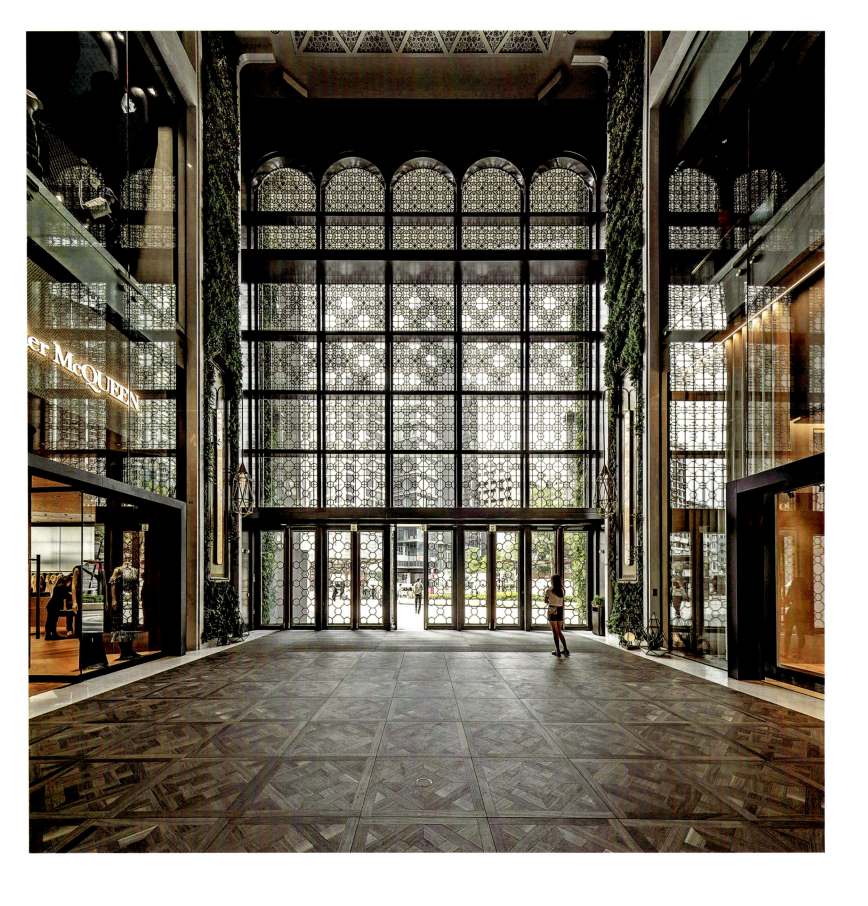

Holiland Concept Store

Design Company
DAS Design Co., Ltd.

Project Designers
DAS Lab

Project Location
China

Site Area
80 m²

No matter in the past, now or in the future, people always keep exploring more dimensions of food, which promotes the continuous iteration and innovation of food production technology. The development of the food industry also brings infinite possibilities for people's eating and living. This symbiotic relationship became the concept of space's inspiration, the designer tries to absorb material from the complexity of the post-industrial era, imagines the scene as a "systematic" production workshop, where the products displayed are more like precise, controlled industrial products.

In this project, creating a mechanical aesthetics space, using the contemporary mainstream media, to take the interior as a medium to deliver the messages from the spirit of Holiland, and to moderate a casual and in-deepth converstation, in a more emotional way, between the brand and the public.

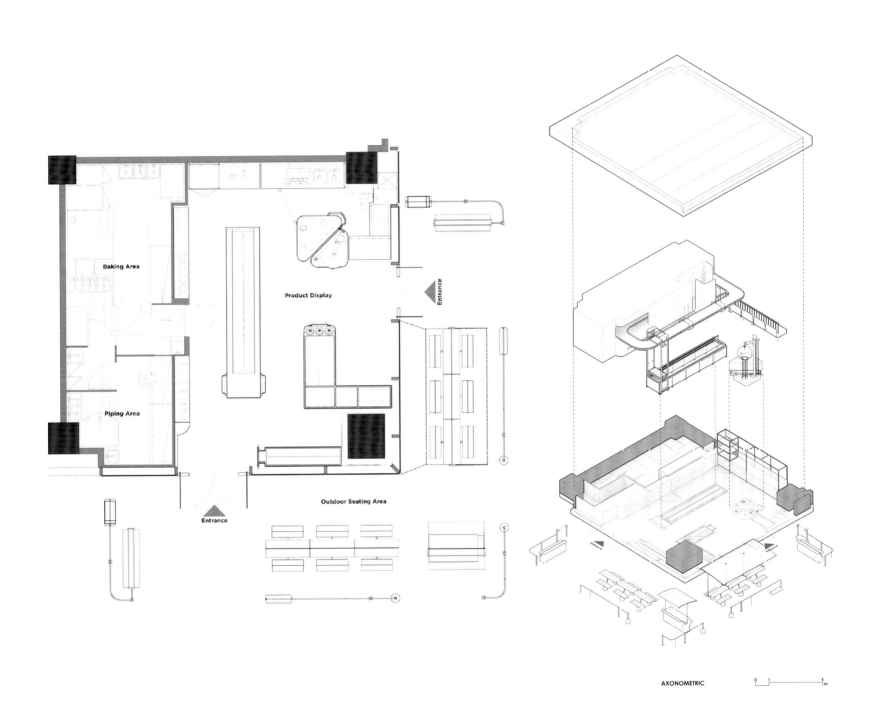

AXONOMETRIC

Magic Box

Design Company
DOMANI Architectural Concepts

Project Designers
Liang Yongzhao

Project Location
Shanghai, China

Site Area
200 m²

The fashion-forward red shape is used to re-display the concept of urban heart. With "the ever-changing commercial space" as its spatial objective, and "integration-separation" as its design language, the magic box provides different display options to build a target venue that revolutionizes customers' knowledge about fashion and design, and to create new possibilities to use different scenes.

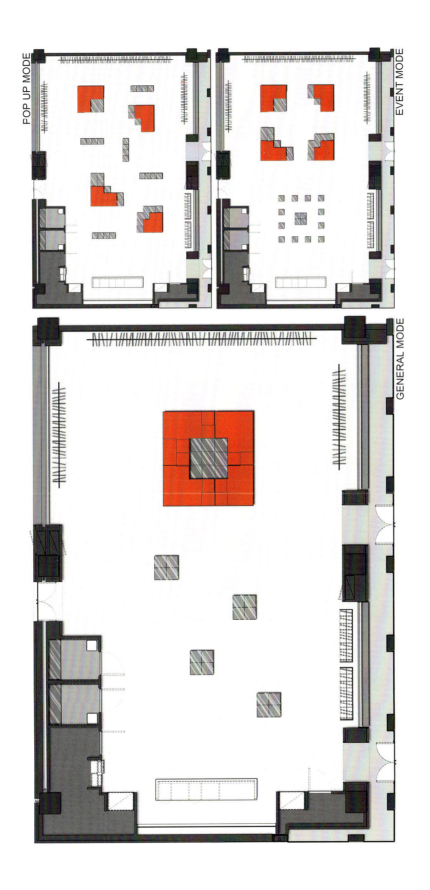

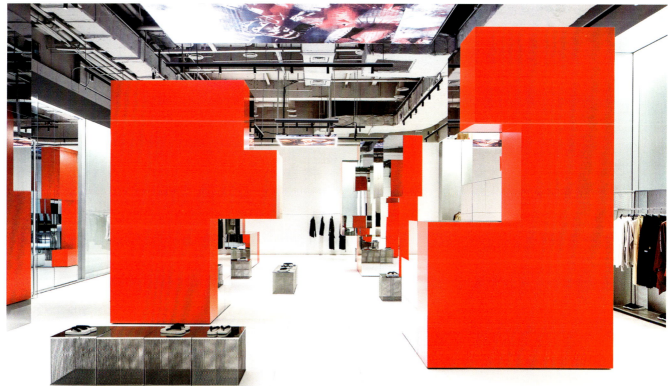

201

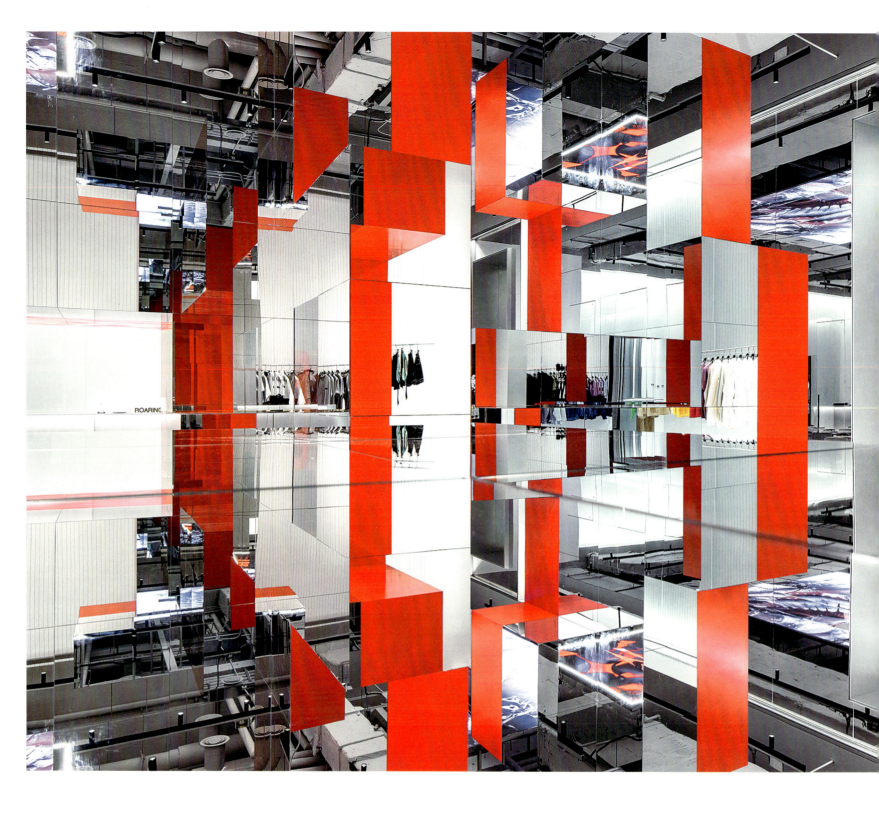

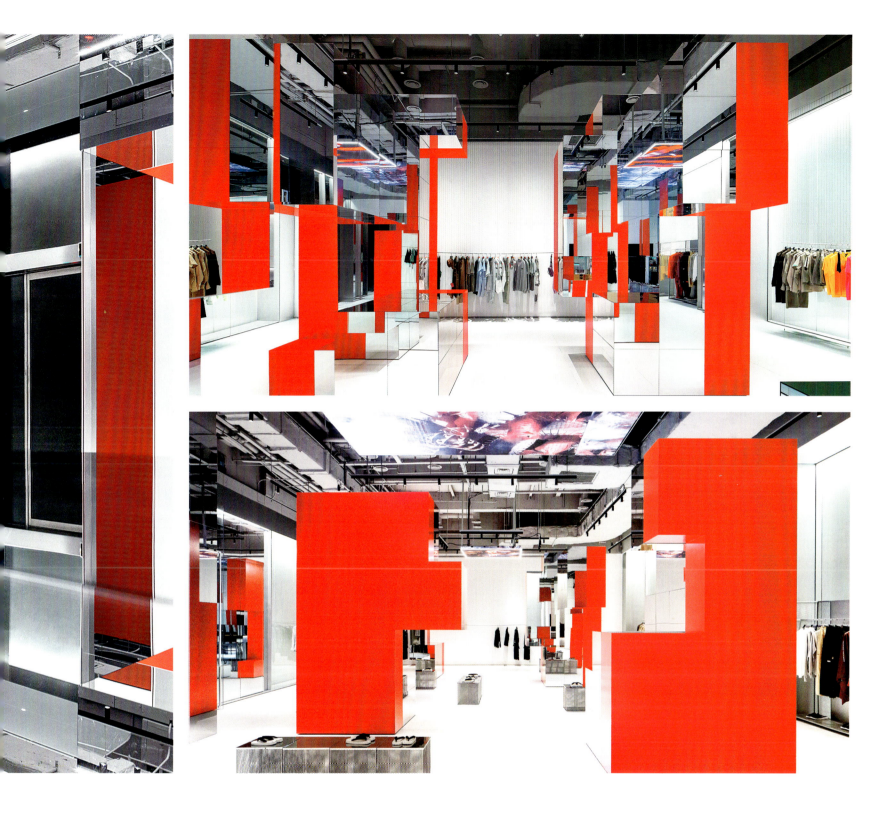

Shopping Space

Honourable Mention

Majimaya Confectionery Tool Shop

Design Company
KAMITOPEN Co., Ltd.

Project Designers
Masahiro Yoshida, Yoshie Ishii

Project Location
Japan

Site Area
198 m²

The theme of this project is "Mold of Happiness". From here, the designer hopes to spread the smile across Japan by making candy.

The client presented a very specific request: 3,000 different types of dessert molds must be displayed in the store, so the designer needed to solve this problem in 200 m² limited space.

Evacuation staircases and protective fences surround the rooms, and 3,000 moulds are placed on a device at the centre of the building. In addition, 3,000 tin boxes have been placed around the mold. By checking the mold with the number on the tin box, customers can choose the mold from the stock.

In addition, in the planning of the building, the floors are connected in a split-level manner, so when choosing the moulds, the client will unconsciously move up and down the floors. This solves the particular problem of the arcade area.

PLAN

Shopping Space

Honourable Mention

Muse Edition

Design Company
New World Development Company Limited

Project Designers
New World Development Company Limited & 1:1

Project Location
Hong Kong, China

Site Area
929 m²

The site was a historical godown terminal called Holt's Wharf in Tsim Sha Tsui from 1910 to 1971. Decades ago, it was situated on top of the harbour as being a dockyard. Since the significance of the architectural character is simply too historic to be neglected, K11 positions the project with the concept of architectural monument, to retain the structural elements. By embracing the beauty of its architectural features.

Inspired by the sailing and dockyard, featured ceiling crystal lightings are purposely redesigned. The use of hand-blowing glass retains an exact shape of the fresnel lens from the lighthouse beacon, casting soft shadows on the floor. The place is transformed into a retail arcade with historical structural elements retained and exposed. For example, the open ceiling without dressed up is exposed to allow a seeing-through concrete waffle ceiling.

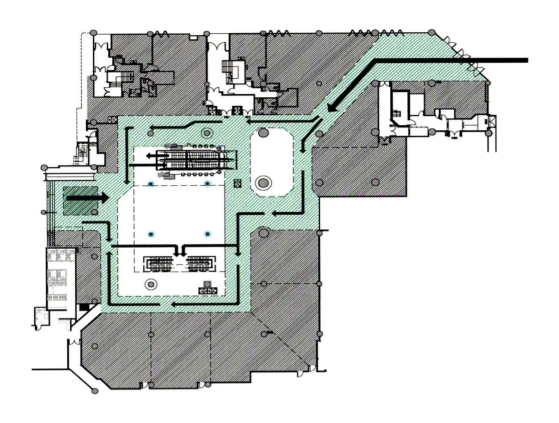
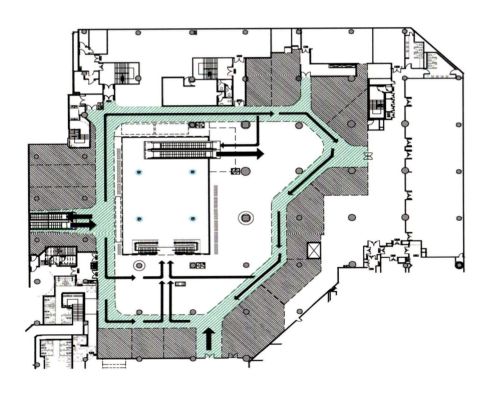

Circulation Analysis on Upper Floor

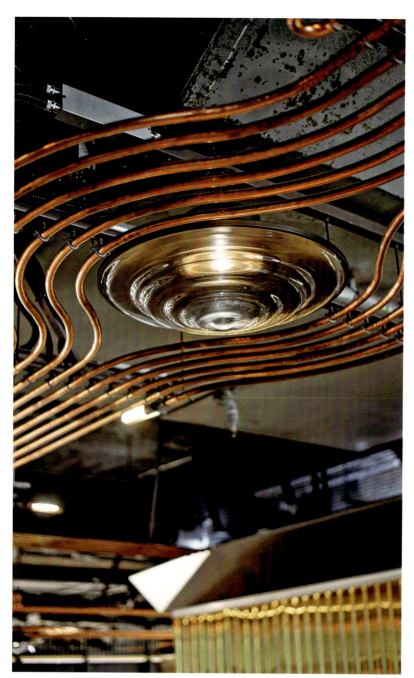

Hotel Space

Gold

Kimpton Da An Hotel

Design Company
Neri&Hu Design and Research Office

Project Designers
Lyndon Neri & Rossana Hu, Laurent Tek, Akrawit Yanpaisan, Chloe Chiu, Federico Salmaso, James Beadnall, Chao Ji, Lara de Pedro, Brian Lo, Junho Jeon, Mona He, Xiaowen Chen, Haiou Xin, Chengju Chang, Jacqueline Yam

Project Location
Taiwan, China

Site Area
8,000 m²

Located in the pristine Da'an district of Taipei, Kimpton Da An Hotel was conceptualized to be an interior sanctuary – an urban retreat that offers calmness and respite from the city's bustling streets and alleys without losing the vibrancy and richness of its unique urban context. The guestrooms offer the most intimate and personal experience of the sanctuary concept. Wooden insertions, expressed as thresholds, sectionalize the room to create in-between spaces. Enclosed in between the thresholds, this space offers a momentary retreat – an introverted space for contemplation.

The challenge for Kimpton Da An was how to convert a residential building into a hotel due to the idiosyncrasies of the plan. To work with the many variances across the room types, bespoke wooden millwork elements were strategically tailored to each room type to create various functions catering to the guests' needs.

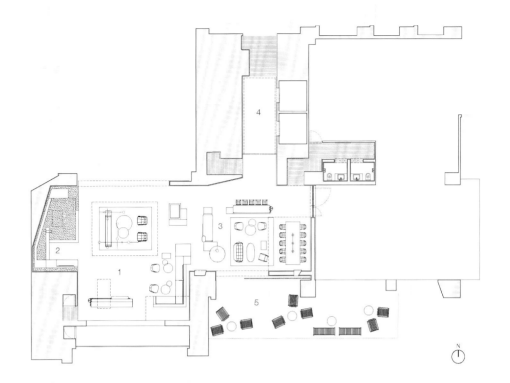

LEVEL 01
1 Lobby & Reception
2 Water feature
3 Lobby lounge
4 Lift Lobby
5 Outdoor terrace

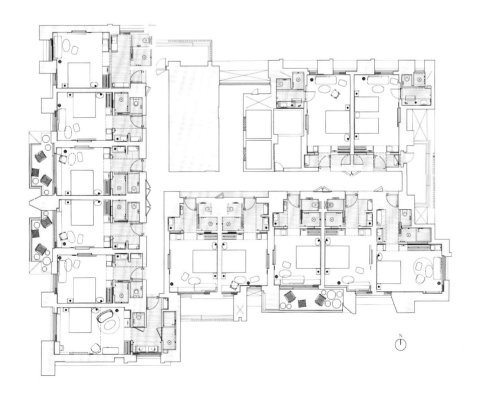

TYPICAL GUESTROOM FLOOR

219

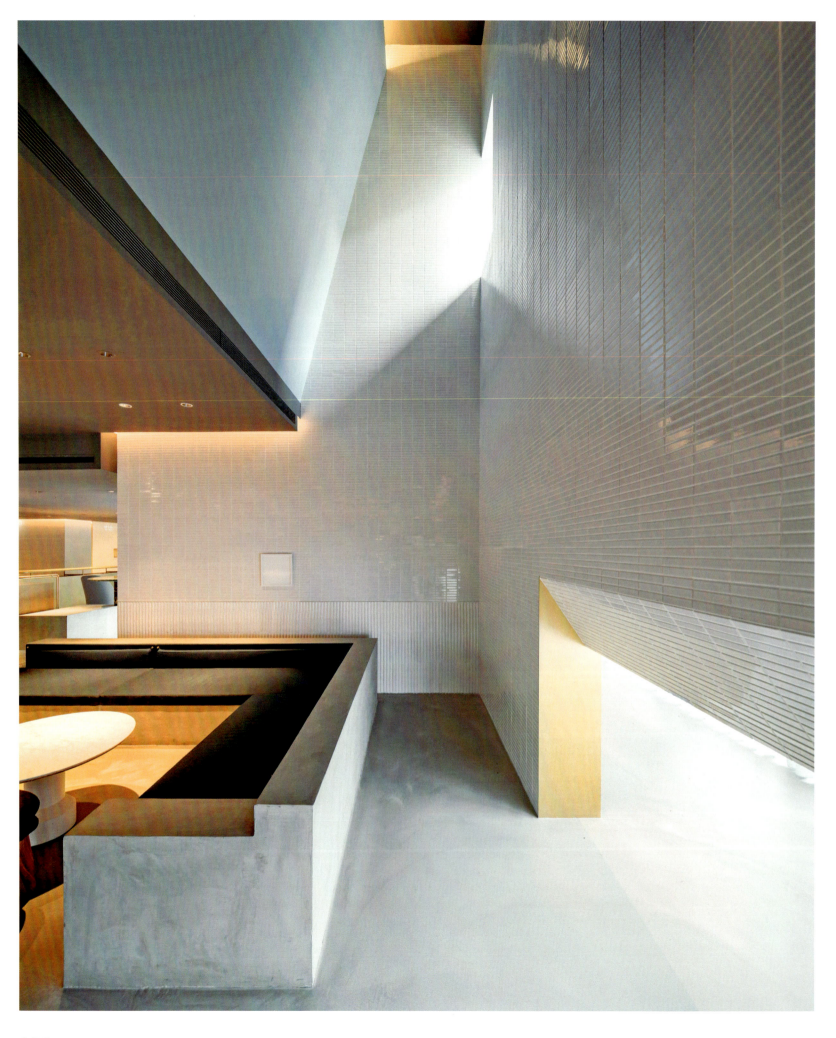

Sincere Hotel

Design Company
Benzhe Design

Project Designers
Janry Jiang, Yao Ruigen, Lin Tong

Project Location
Jiangsu, China

Site Area
1,280 m²

This project is located at the foot of Nanchan Temple in Wuxi, among a cluster of civilian houses near a Qing Dynasty famous bridge and ancient canal of the Qing Dynasty, hence the name 'Nanchan Guanshui'. With the changing times and urban regeneration, the designers have deconstructed the hotel to reveal the new meaning of the building, while at the same time passing on the essence of the historical and cultural heritage. The design is based on history, but is also based on nature, bringing harmony between architecture, people and nature.

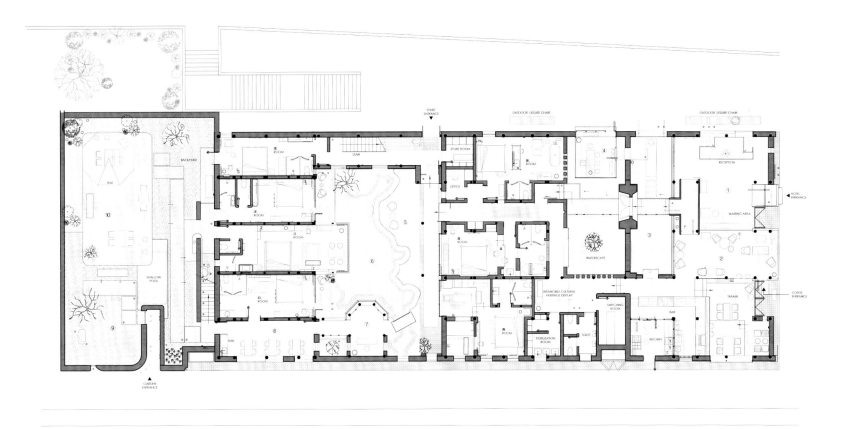

THE FIRST FLOOR PLAN

01 THE HOTEL LOBBY
02 COFFEE
03 WATERFALL
04 VIEWING TEA ROOM
05 CHINESE COURTYARD
06 ORNAMENTAL FISH POND
07 PAVILION
08 SHARED SPACE
09 DRY LANDSCAPE
10 BARBECUE

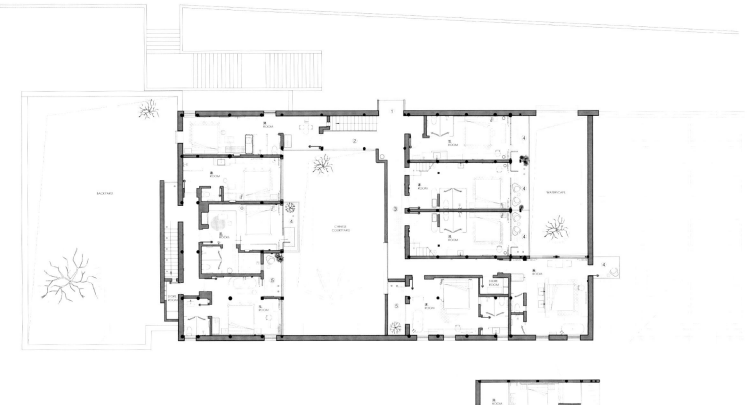

THE SECOND FLOOR PLAN

01 VIEWFINDER
02 GLASS WALKWAY
03 SUNSHINE CORRIDOR
04 VIEWING BALCONY
05 INNER BALCONY

The Sukhothai Shanghai

Design Company
Neri&Hu Design and Research Office

Project Designers
Lyndon Neri & Rossana Hu, Laurent Tek, Akrawit Yanpaisan, Chloe Chiu, Federico Salmaso, James Beadnall, Chao Ji, Lara de Pedro, Brian Lo, Junho Jeon, Mona He, Xiaowen Chen, Haiou Xin, Chengju Chang, Jacqueline Yam

Project Location
Shanghai, China

Site Area
24,000 m²

Like its predecessor in Bangkok, the Sukhothai hotel in Shanghai aspires to encapsulate the essences of Thai culture — a profound spiritual compassion, a refined aesthetic sense, and a deep connection with nature. The design concept of the project is based on the concern for the general negative situation of people in Asian metropolises — feeling crowded, psychologically fragile, longing to get close to nature, hoping to find breathing space and rejuvenate. Therefore, the project hopes to be an oasis in the city, close to nature in all aspects. This is particularly evident in the design of gardens. An extended garden path leads the guests to their own retreats. At the entry to the lobby, stacked gray terrazzo slabs create an illusion of a floating staircase. With the woven latticework of the lantern as a backdrop, custom bronze and glass ball pendant fixtures are strategically placed, so that guests feel as if they are walking in and amongst the glowing lights.

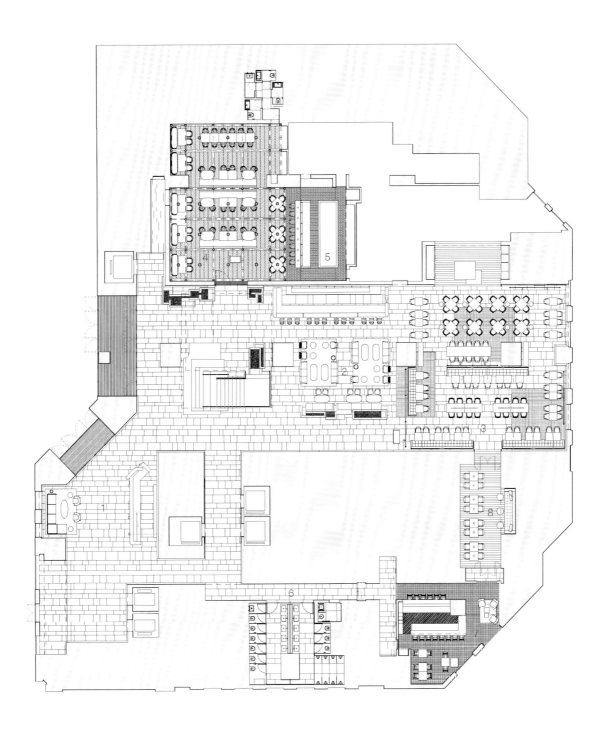

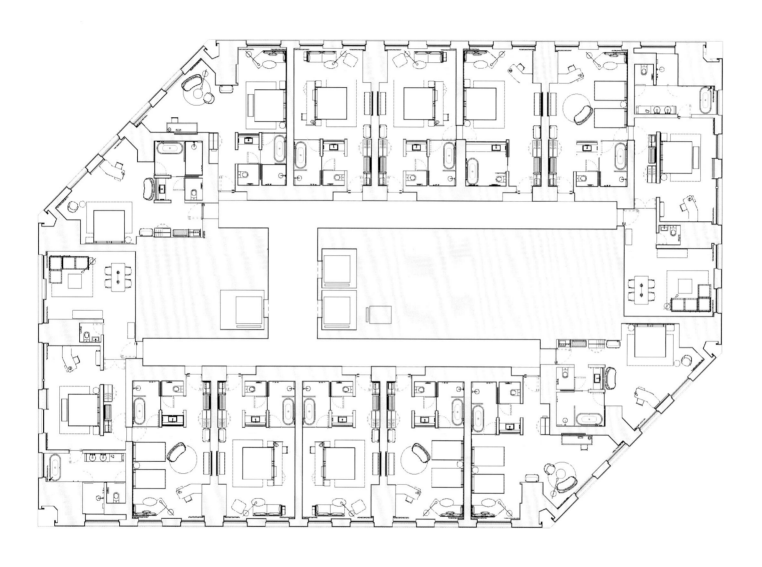

Hotel Anteroom Naha

Design Company
UDS Ltd.

Project Designers
UDS Ltd.

Project Location
Japan

Site Area
2,625 m²

Hotel Anteroom Naha strives to bring excitement to its neighbourhood by introducing Okinawa art and culture. Inspired by the image of a blank canvas, the simple interior design encourages the guests to take a closer look at the artworks exhibited throughout the hotel. The facade, interior and furniture were designed in close collaboration with artists to turn the space itself a piece of art. The gallery is a place for upcoming creators can express themselves through their latest work, and guests are welcome purchase the displayed artworks from both the exhibition area and their guest-rooms to take home.

The minimalist design and decor are meant to inspire travellers to refresh, relax and prepare for their next adventure. The cruise ship-inspired architecture and building materials highlights the harbour-side location and its layout allows guests to overlook the ocean from anywhere, at any time.

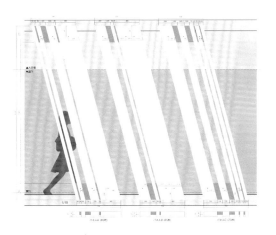
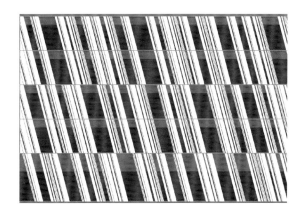

ELEVATION | DETAIL

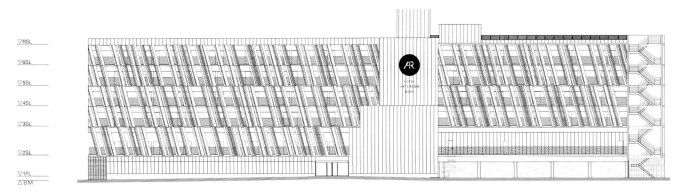

ELEVATION

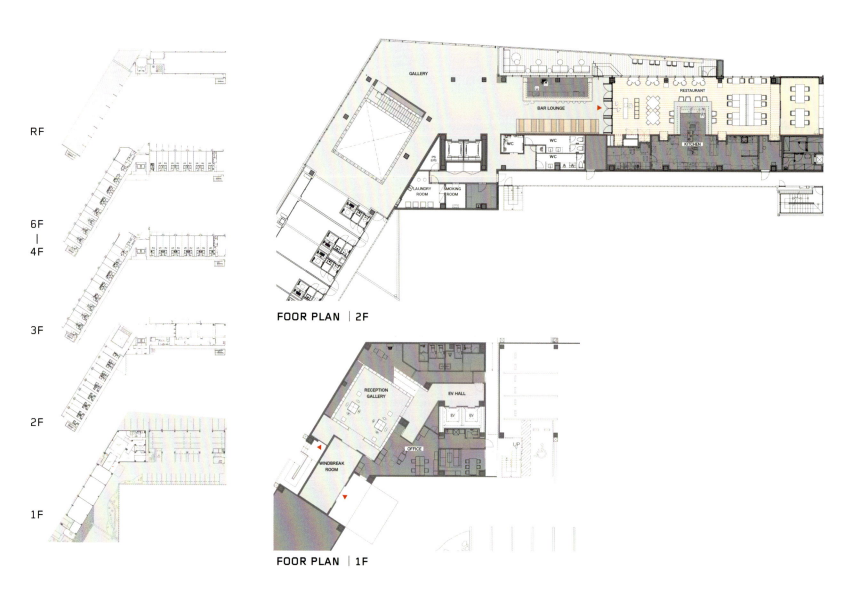

The Westin in Zhongshan

Design Company
Yang Bangsheng & Associates Group

Project Designers
Yang Bangsheng, Chen Bohua, Wang Qin, Hu Zhaozhen

Project Location
Guangdong, China

Site Area
39,000 m²

Standing as the landmark of the Zhongshan Ancient Town, the capital of China's decorative lighting industry, the Westin Zhongshan Guzhen is an essential facility to serve the local lighting expo centre and international lighting exhibitions. Based on Westin's natural and vigorous style, the designer conveys the warmness, brightness, hope and other cultural connotations behind light fittings by exploring the core culture of the "Light Capital" and using various lamp elements creatively. The hotel, which values environmental protection and regional characteristics, does not only serve as a new urban cultural name card, but also functions as an international display window to the charm of China's lighting industry capital.

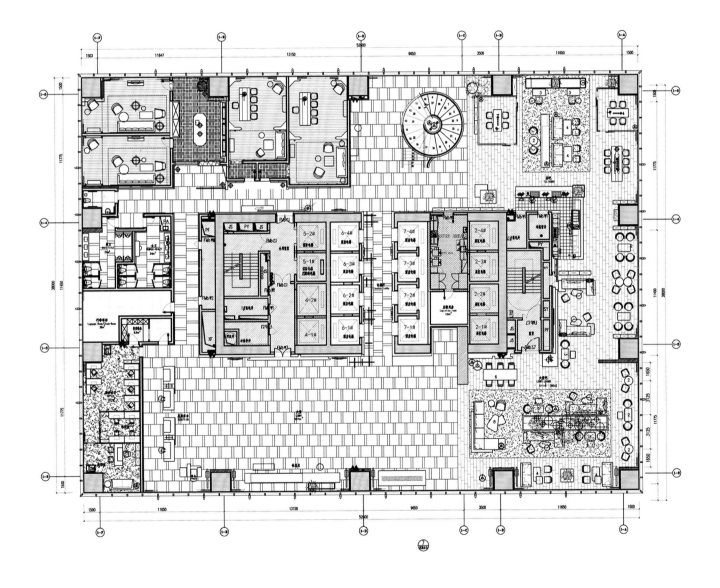

247

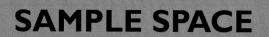

Sample Space

Gold

Obsidian Villa

Design Company
Sunny Neuhaus Partnership

Project Designers
Wang Xiaofeng, Lu Fengzuo, Chen Weiyi

Project Location
Guangdong, China

Site Area
885 m²

Designer has been inspired by the mysterious obsidian. Through the analysis of high net worth business group, designer deeply excavates the living pursuit and taste of the residents, and fully shows the experience of the space with the sense of obsidian, so as to create a high-end hotel and club style resort lake house for the residents.

Bold design into the concept of leisure vacation, art movement, and comprehensive shows the tension of space design under the metropolitan style, highlighting the mysterious, noble, sharp, capable aspect of the city upstart. Bring different interest to life space and grade space. Create a high-end living scene with light grey, leather and advanced stone material. The overall design concept is calm and understated while details are highlighted. It fully demonstrates the stability and nobility of the space and its owner.

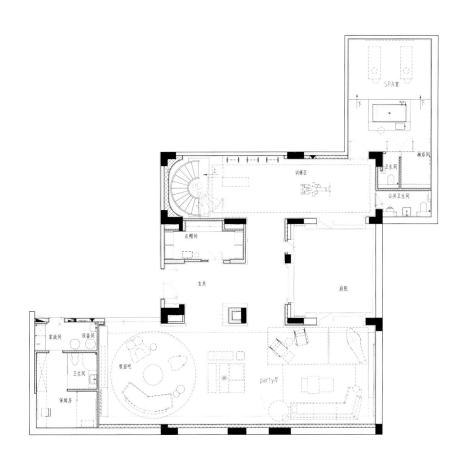

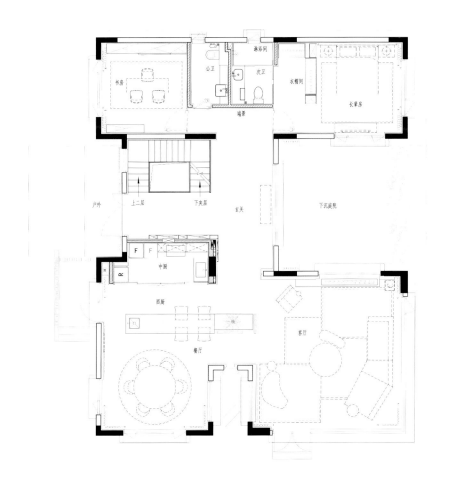

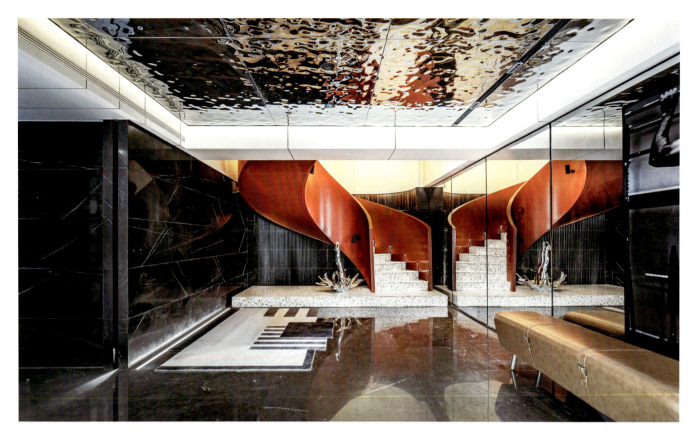

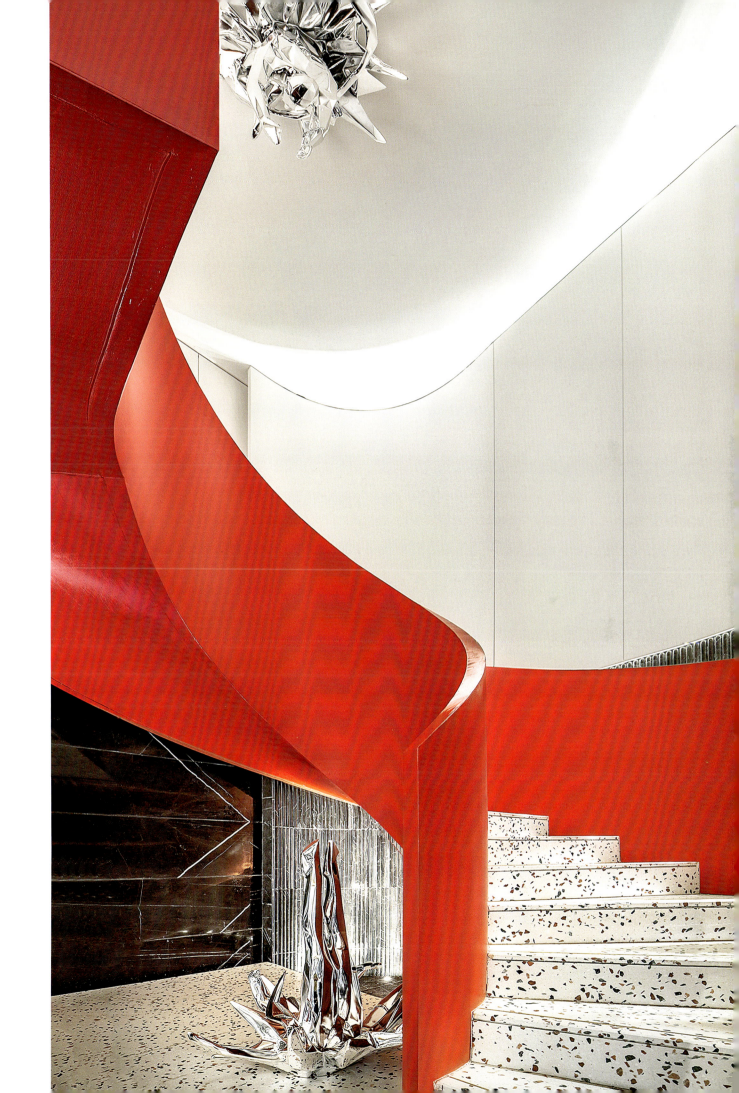

Silent

Design Company
C&C Design Co., Ltd.

Project Designers
Peng Zheng, Zhang Bo, Xu Shuxin

Project Location
Guangdong, China

Site Area
230 m²

Located in the north of Shaoguan, the project is separated from the hustle and bustle of the city. Facing China Danxia Mountain, the building follows the slope of the mountain and grows in nature. Through the semi-permeable camphor paper, sunlight sprinkles and creates the dim silence. The natural wood fragrance is catalyzed by light and shadow to permeates the space, which makes the beauty of the object itself extremely magnified. Staying in the villa, you will feel that the potential emotions of being nostalgic and returning to nature have all been compensated.

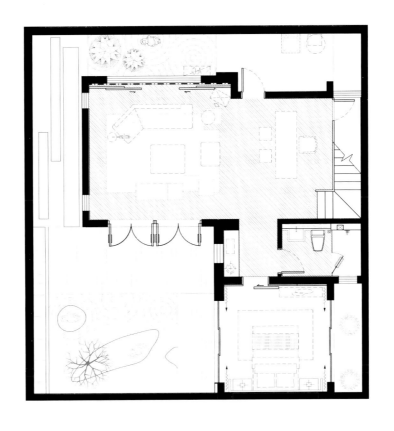
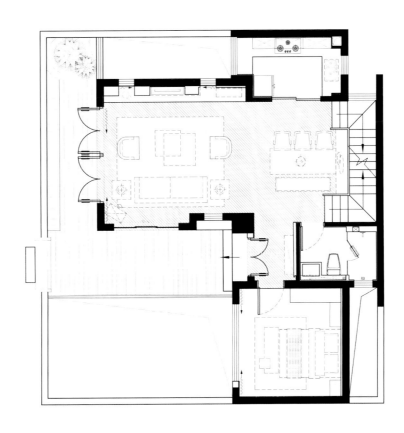

259

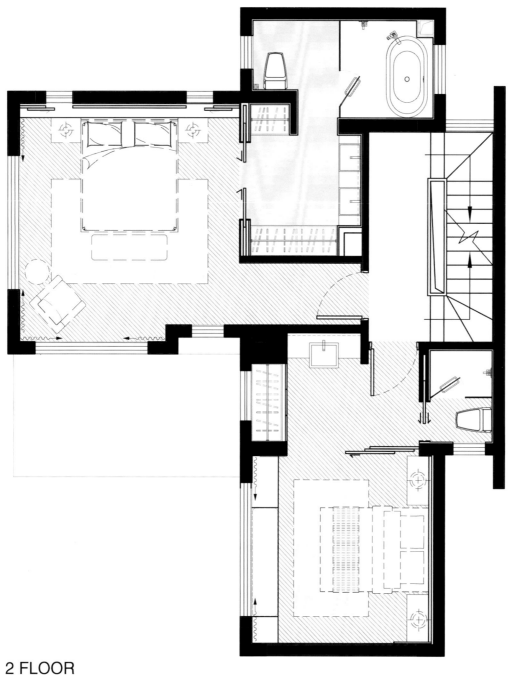

2 FLOOR

Sample Space

Silver

The Entrance

Design Company
Danny Cheng Interiors Ltd.

Project Designers
Danny Cheng

Project Location
Hong Kong, China

Site Area
153 m²

The starting point for the project is its unique environmental conditions, with sweeping views of the sea and plenty of natural light. Therefore, light wood colour materials, natural stone and the same colour materials were selected to decorate the apartment into a bright and warm interior space, with curved lights, flowers and various customized details, create a unique taste of life by a simple style. Users can relax themselves in a simple and quiet environment and fully enjoy the natural beauty.

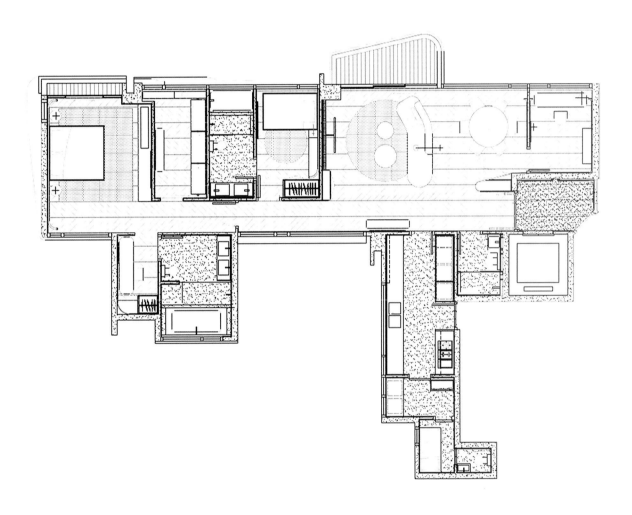

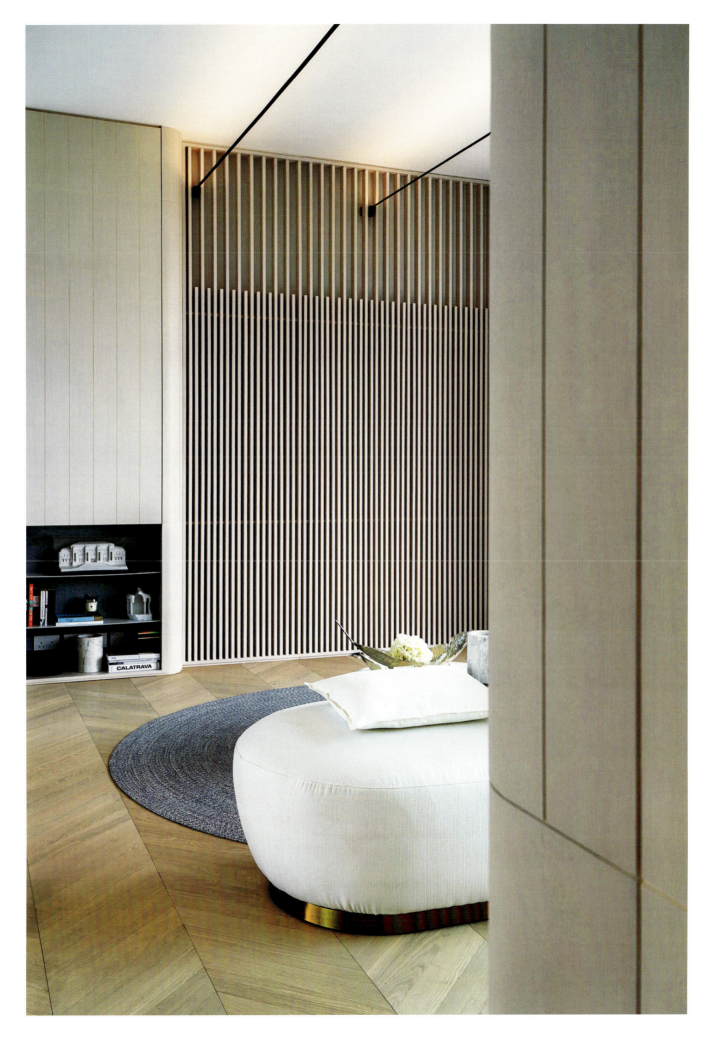

Sample Space

Bronze

Jiangshan Wanli Aerial Villa

Design Company
Symmetry Design

Project Designers
Chen Henghuan

Project Location
Zhejiang, China

Site Area
208 m²

The project is located in front of the Central Park in Qinzhou District, Ningbo City, so the relationship between "residence and park" has become the most important design topic in this case. The design makes the living room face the park directly, integrating the interior space with the park. Therefore, the residents will feel that they are almost living in the park. Residents can surround a fireplace which is added on the wall facing the park with their friends and relatives to keep warm while viewing the landscape, enjoying life in nature. It could be seen as the most beautiful scene in the space.

Simple and pure space shows elegant demeanor. High-quality materials and the style of space echo each other. Concise spatial layer and beautiful lines of the home style express the connotation of design.

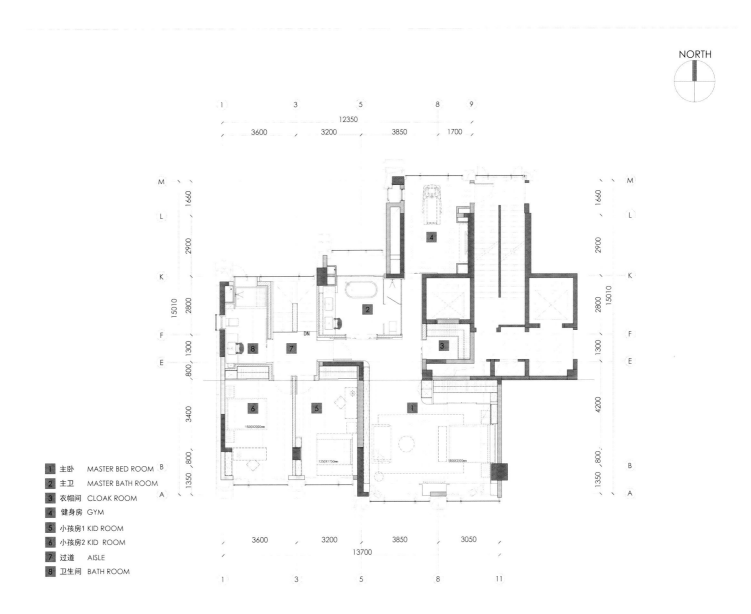

1	客厅 LIVING AREA
2	餐厅 DINING AREA
3	书房 STUDY ROOM
4	卧室 BED ROOM1
5	卫生间 BATH ROOM
6	阳台 BALCONY
7	厨房 KITCHEN

Connaught Serviced Apartments

Design Company
Matter Limited

Project Designers
Joanna Mok, Grace Tsang

Project Location
Hong Kong, China

Site Area
101 m²

Connaught Serviced Apartments is located in the prestigious Harbour-front Tower in Sai Ying Pun, Hong Kong. The project responds to the character of Hong Kong and conveys a strong sense of workplace style and refined stylistic aspirations. The project exudes a modern, understated elegance through lines and geometric patterns. A dark, masculine decorative approach creates a stately studio atmosphere, while balancing the ambience with light wood flooring. The home is finished in royal blue, enhancing the decorative qualities and giving it more personality than the usual workplace.

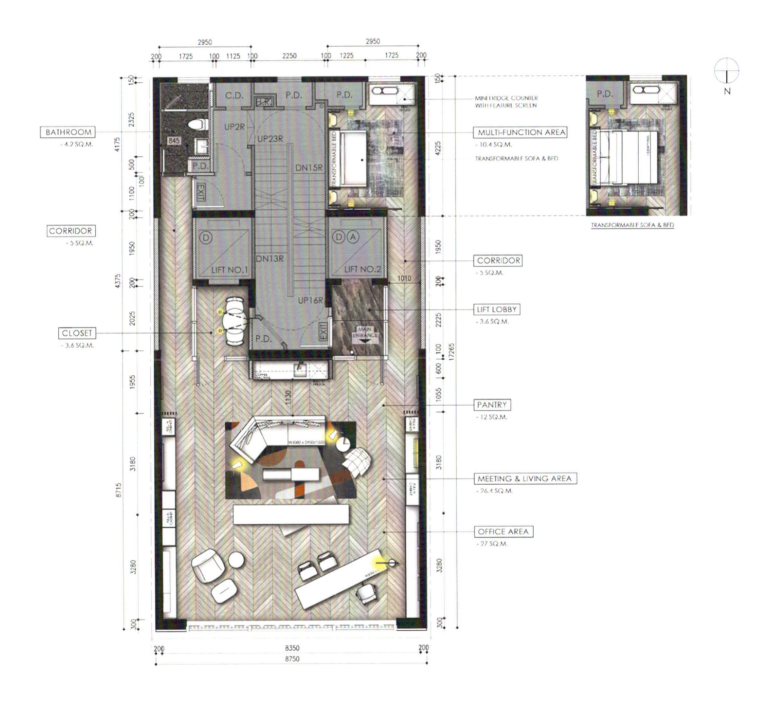

Sample Space

Honourable Mention

Sunac Elegant West Garden

Design Company
Shenzhen Huomo International Design

Project Designers
Xiong Yanhua

Project Location
Guangdong, China

Site Area
248 m²

The Song Dynasty was called the "Eastern Renaissance" by western scholars. It makes the pinnacle of Chinese classical arts. This gentleman's style and manner, the rich culture accumulated through times, and that elegant artistic temperament are all displayed in living style and furnishing aesthetics in this project. It refers to the style of the Song Dynasty, inheriting its inner spirits yet not following its format. The solid and void in between space has its own rhythm, floating around with one's heart and the changing of seasons, thus transforming the virtual space into an actual life. Artistic landscaping language not only just showcases the cultural context of this project, but also brings unique personality to it. In a contemporary way, it interprets the Chinese aesthetics that reflect people's ideal vision of an Oriental style life, bringing an ancient touch of creativity to the modern life.

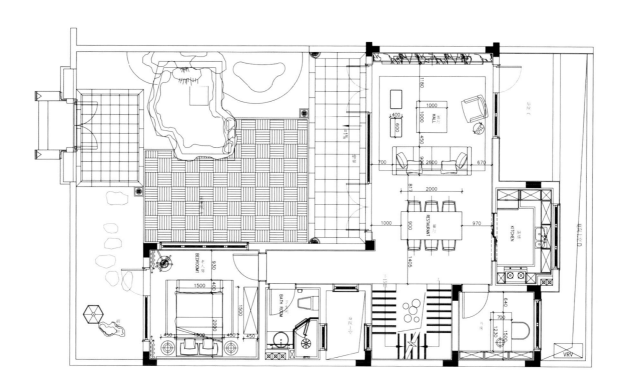

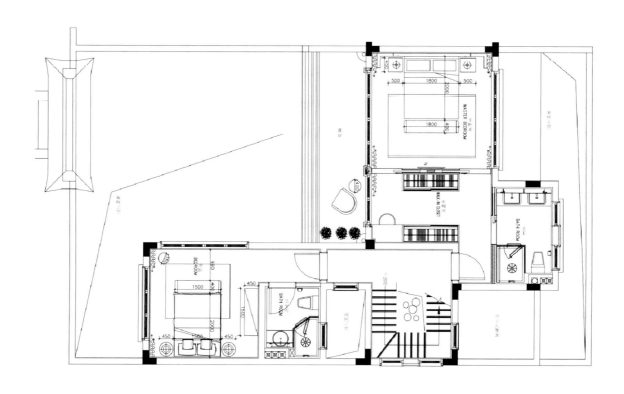

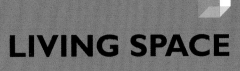

Sanctuary of the Soul

Design Company
UNI-X Associates

Project team
UNI-X Associates team

Project Location
Jiangsu, China

Site Area
130 m²

The client is a director so that his job makes him pursue the spiritual life. He wants to jump out of the thinking world, changes states and calms down in a peaceful household environment. Original space has three bedrooms, two bathrooms, one living room and one dining room. Since there are many load-bearing walls, designers have to build atmosphere with accessories design instead of change the whole structure.

The design style returns to simplicity, pursues the integration of tranquillity and scenery, introduces landscape appropriately, adds poetry and vitality, takes lighting as the breakthrough point, and waits for the free growth of emotion in the space between light and shadow. The layout structure preserves the living requirements.
One of the original three bedrooms is retained, and the others are changed into a cloakroom and a meditation room. Without the demand of sky lanterns, only four ceiling lights are reserved for the basic lighting of the space, while other indirect lighting is adopted. The natural light from the balcony and the table lamps in the bedrooms are warm light sources to match the tone of the space, seemingly faint but in fact a reflection of the spirit of inner certainty.

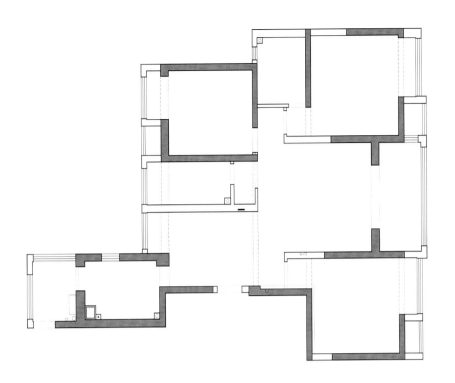
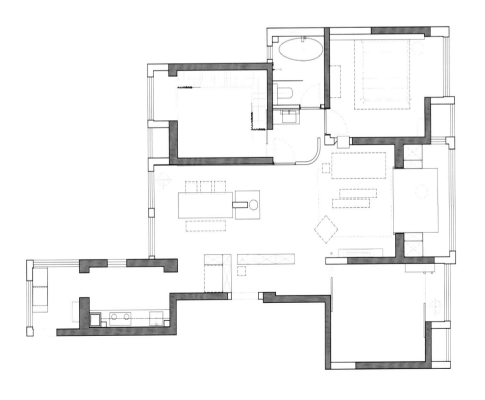

Living Space

Silver

The Home for a Brand New Start

Design Company
PONE Architecture

Project Designers
Ming Leung

Project Location
Guangdong, China

Site Area
123 m²

This is a renovation project. The owner is a professional woman who needs to take care of her children independently. It is important for them to improve efficiency by time and space. Before the renovation, the effective utilization rate of the house was only 55%. Limited space for her daughter to grow up and space for her hobbies.

After transformation, space utilization rate increases, by reorganizing functions distribution, extending living space, designing hobbies area, and using the vacant space to be a guest room in a composite way. We exchange space for life time, improve life quality and take all-round needs into account.

Plan before renovation

The transformed floor plan

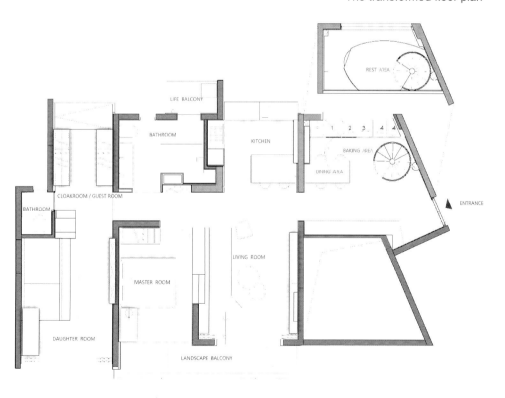

Grosvenor Residence

Design Company
Lim & Lu Design Limited

Project Designers
Vincent Lim, Elaine Lu, Joyce Ho, Quincy Chung

Project Location
Hong Kong, China

Site Area
167 m²

Grosvenor residence was designed as a refurbishment with a fresh natural touch to bring back the 'homely' element of the space. The occupants are a couple (one Japanese and one English) and their children, both of whom love nature. The designer therefore wanted to incorporate natural elements into the design. The neutral tones of the accessories and the variety of greenery that adorn the interior of the space are vibrant and lively, blurring the boundaries between the interior and exterior. The use of wooden slats and rattan creates a rich sense of texture and is in keeping with the overall clean and simple aesthetic. The original small windows have been transformed into large antique glass windows in order to bring in maximum natural light. The above elements work in synergy to take this home out of the concrete jungle.

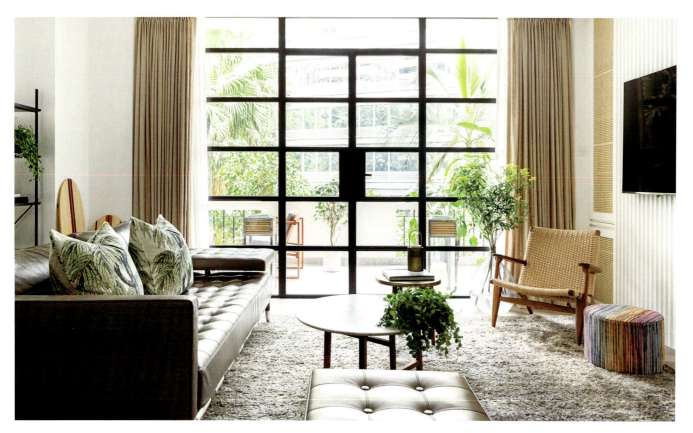

Living Space

Honourable Mention

House in Minohshinmachi

Design Company
Yasuyuki Kitamura

Project Designers
Yasuyuki Kitamura

Project Location
Japan

Site Area
210 m²

This project is located in a new town with a rich natural environment in the northernmost part of Minoh City, Osaka Prefecture. The client is a young couple who were looking for a house to live with nature.

The building is set against Minooyama Mountain. Deep eaves of the light roof extend the interior space, while nested nooks and crannies provide a vague space. In addition, a pair of windows visually brings the exterior scenery into the centre of the building. Large skylights let the mottled tree shadows and the blue sky reflect into the interior. The curtains on the outside block unnecessary sunlight and sight. The two main pillars give a sense of security and create a spacious interior. The completed building blends harmoniously with the environment, which makes people feel that it is a part of nature, rather than separating the natural environment as a landscape.

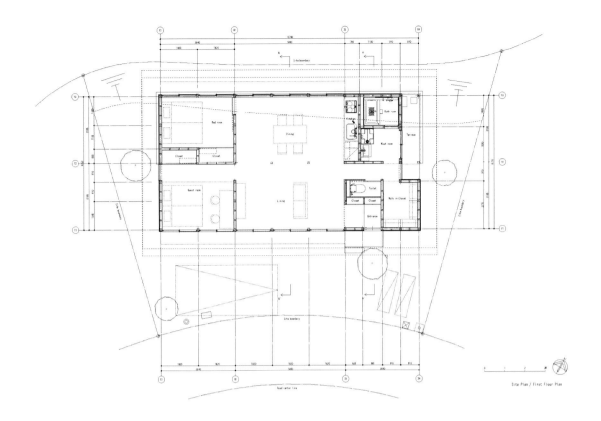

Site Plan / First Floor Plan

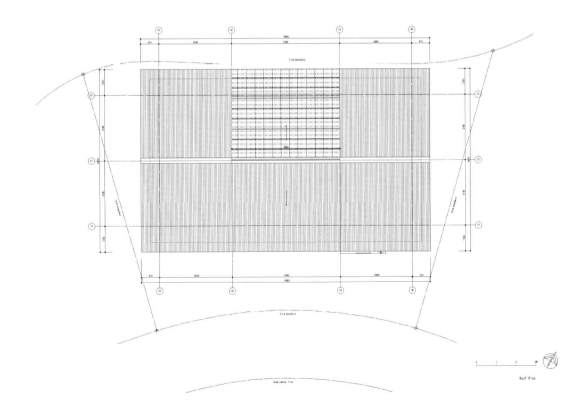

Roof Plan

Living Space

Honourable Mention

Mount Pavilia

Design Company
COMODO Interior & Furniture Design Co., Ltd.

Project Designers
Alain Wong, Shawn Wong

Project Location
Hong Kong, China

Site Area
158 m²

The residence Mount Pavilia in Clearwater Bay is a space designed in harmony with nature for a family of four. The team used a minimalist but warm decorating and furnishing style with a feature ceiling design in the living room. Wood paneling and grid lines on the ceiling and the wall create a clean, straight finish to highlight the area underneath and differentiate the function area. Meanwhile, a curve and bronzed trims are subtly applied on the display shelf, cabinet, partition…etc., which further balance the richness and details yet create a calm and peaceful space to enjoy family time. Master bedroom and study are continuing the colour scheme of the living room with a light grey wallpaper to smoothen and soften the restful sleeping area. Meanwhile, son's bedroom chooses a black and walnut colour to go with the cement textured wallpaper to make it look chic on its own.

LAYOUT PLAN
SCALE: 1:75

SMALL LIVING SPACE

Axis House

Design Company
LCGA Design

Project Designers
Chiu Kai-Chen, Huang Cheng-Yuan

Project Location
Taiwan, China

Site Area
73.5 m²

Square, circle, and lines of light construct a geometric dining space, from which the axes of life originate. Iron display shelves exhibit greenery and memory of life, and lights of x, y, and z dimensions attract the lines of sight of the entire space. Basic geometric elements are piled into volumes, with hidden functionalities embedded within. The combination of various elements produces a leisure space where people can easily interact.

Large white and warm wash stone tiles carry on childhood memory, and the curvature of the humble cement wall creates with light fixtures gentle gradient of light, giving corners in the space rich variations of light and shadow. The folding door of the study with windows at top can freely convert the functionality of the compact space, allowing contemporary and soothing colors to lay down the axes of a leisure life.

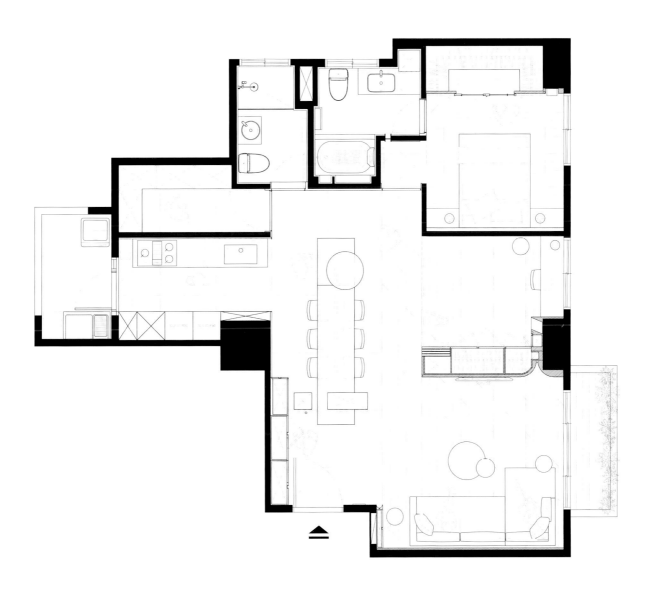

323

Layers

Design Company
Dig Design

Project Designers
Zhong Zhiqian, Gu Zhenyi

Project Location
Taiwan, China

Site Area
50 m²

Since the house-owner's child is still in pre-school age, independent children's room are not necessary to this family. Therefore, designer uses "transformation" in the children's room, making this area children's play area and guest room. In addition, designer takes advantage of the height of the house to make a raised floor and set the storage function down to keep the wall blank. It also serves as an image to breathe in time in a fast-paced city.

Small Living Space

Bronze

La Parfumeuse

Design Company
PTang Studio Limited

Project Designers
Philip Tang, Brian Ip

Project Location
Singapore

Site Area
72.4 m²

As narration of lifestyle and spatial qualities of a perfumer, elegance is the key for the two-bedroom unit. Beige colour tone and soft leather touch infiltrates the scent of elegance and subtlety of a dainty bottle of perfume. The use of lacquer and metal is in marked contrast to the soft leather surface.

In the living room, the shelf with staggering layers acts as partition between it and the study room and enhance the spacious quality of the living room. More importantly, selection of curvy furniture and lighting with a pinch of colourful elements adds on a vogue and playful touch, like a bottle of classy elegant perfume.

LAYOUT PLAN
1:50

333

Savour Dwelling

Design Company
Otherwhere Studio Limited

Project Designers
Udo Lam, Frankie Chao

Project Location
Hong Kong, China

Site Area
73 m²

In the city with skyscraper skylines, the breathtaking scenery of sunlight and mountains could be a luxurious desire. The combination of a range of natural dark woods and stucco color tones materials emphasizes the light and shadow. A wooden frame box decorated at window sill allows the outside greenery integrated perfectly into the house.

The space will have different expressions when the time passes, resident could enjoy the movement of sunlight and the variety of mountains, at the same time, the mild wood matched with the soft warm lighting creates a diverse and soothing living vibe for resident to relax and collect himself.

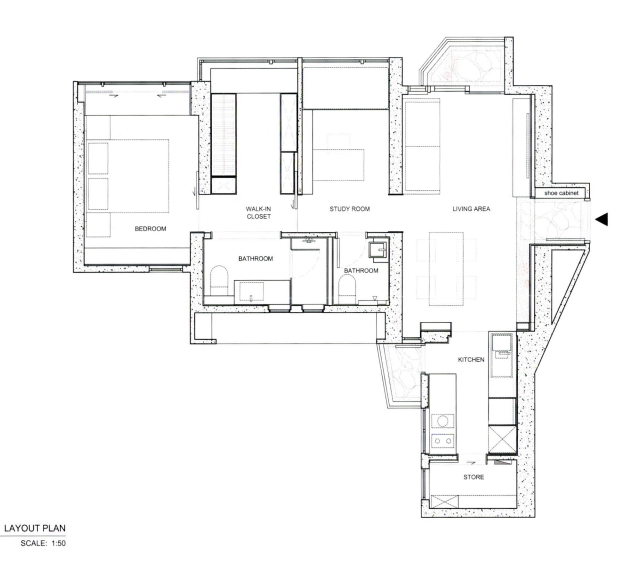

Between Mountains and Sea

Design Company
Degree Design

Project Designers
Zeng Zhihao

Project Location
Taiwan, China

Site Area
43 m²

The project is located on the northern coast of Taiwan. The arch in the entrance is to symbolize a ceremony. To cleanse the soul, escape from the hustle and bustle of life and find the true self after passing through layers of mountains and tunnels. The designer simplifies the material, tries to return the essence of life and respond to nature with humility. The dome shape ceiling implies the stacked hills, and the artwork corresponds to the endless ocean outside the window. Between reality and fiction, the invisible horizontal and vertical axis and the flow line create a different lifestyle.

WORK SPACE

Work Space

Gold

Xige Estate

Design Company
Saussure Architects

Project Designers
Li Wanhong, Ren Xiangdong

Project Location
Ningxia, China

Site Area
25,000 m²

The design of the whole winery is flexible, the production area with efficiency as the priority is calmer and tougher in spatial form, which is reflected as a modern power. The other functional areas mainly for visiting and leisure are slightly soft and calm, showing a kind of inspiration for nature to all things.

In terms of indoor treatment, it is more "sustainable" oriented. A large number of Helan Mountain stones enter the space in the original shape, forming the internal landscape. The terrazzo processed and polished by Helan Mountain stone can be seen everywhere in the space, exuding a warm and delicate temperament. In addition to making the doors wait to be reconstructed by light and shadow, the recyclable insect-eroded teak also constructs the top structure of the reading area, responding to the rolling Helan Mountain.

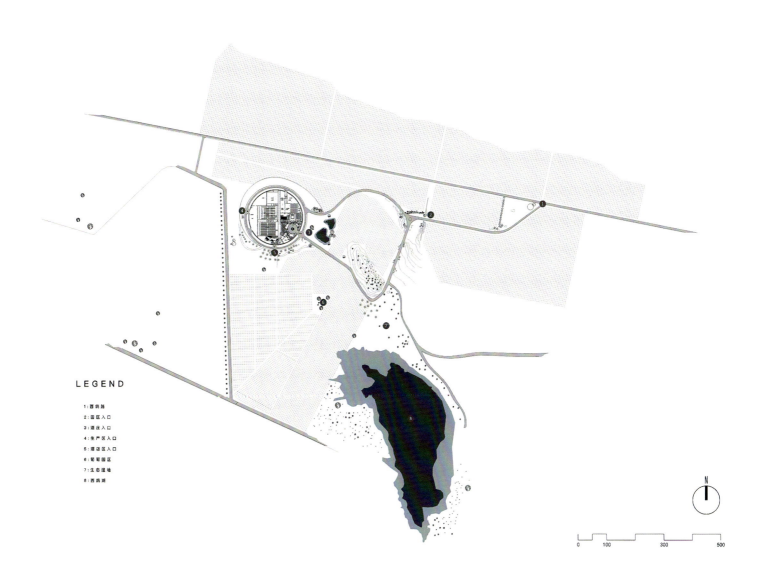

Poly Raise Space

Design Company
BEING Architects

Project Designers
Dai Jiaming, Guo Yuan, Feng Yi, Chen Jie, Chen Xiaocong, Jiang Jianlun, Li Yuqing

Project Location
Guangdong, China

Site Area
2,700 m²

Raise Space is a new comprehensive space brand launched by Poly South China, which is located in the high-rise office building. Different from traditional renovation, as a new space brand, Ruisi workshop aims to create a diversified sharing environment in high-rise buildings, explore possibility of social mode in the future. As the way of traditional spatial layout can no longer meet the new needs, immersive experience and flexible scenes are more in line with the new social model. Raise strives to create a space integrating office, business, entertainment, leisure and art, including a series of composite functions. The open urban landscape on all sides of the standard floor in the tower is the biggest feature of the site. The design hopes to enlarge this feature, maximize the external landscape resources, introduce it into interior, overlap with the interior landscape, and create a city kaleidoscope, a sky garden of contemporary art in the high-rise.

The design attempts to implant a new brand installation in the space and recreate the whole standard floor, and take it as the space carrier to create a flowing and inclusive space; which can overlap and connect various scenes, meet with various people, things, environments and values under "We Media" era, and become a dynamic and inclusive social place.

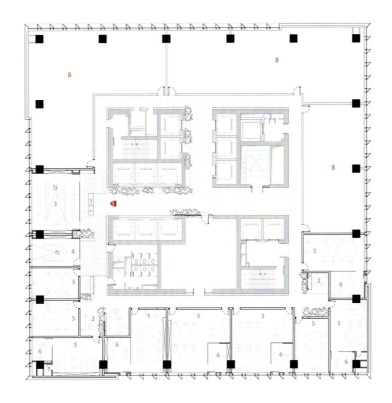

▶	主入口	Main entrance
1.	前台	Reception
2.	休闲区	Leisure area
3.	大会议室	Large meeting room
4.	会议室	Meeting room
5.	办公室	Office
6.	经理室	Manager's office
7.	储物间	Storage
8.	独立办公	Independent office

34th FLOOR

▶	入口	Entrance
▶	主入口	Main entrance
1.	前台	Reception
2.	洽谈区	Meeting area
3.	共享办公区	Co-working area
4.	路演区	Roadshow area
5.	瑜伽	Yoga
6.	操房	Gymnastics room
7.	重型器材区	Heavy equipment area
8.	书吧	Book bar
9.	休闲水吧	water bar
10.	淋浴区	Shower area

33th FLOOR

359

The PolyCuboid Office Building

Design Company
KTX archiLAB

Project Designers
Tetsuya Matsumoto, Motoaki Takeuchi, Farid Ziani

Project Location
Japan

Site Area
621 m²

The PolyCuboid is the new headquarter building for TIA. The volume is composed of an interlace of three cuboid shapes creating intersections, voids, and space units. The cuboids superposition allows a richer space syntax including interior and exterior terraces, an atrium, several seating spaces, and a clear yet richer functional distribution of spaces and connections.

The metallic structure of the building dissolves into the diverse blocs of the composition. The pillars and beams vanish from the space syntax, and the space is full of the aesthetics of sculpture.

1F

2F

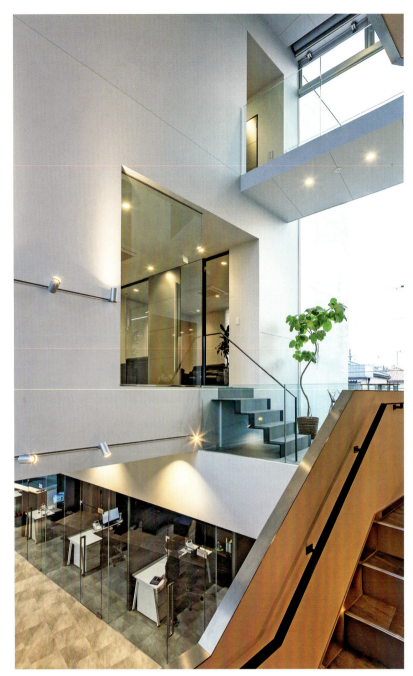

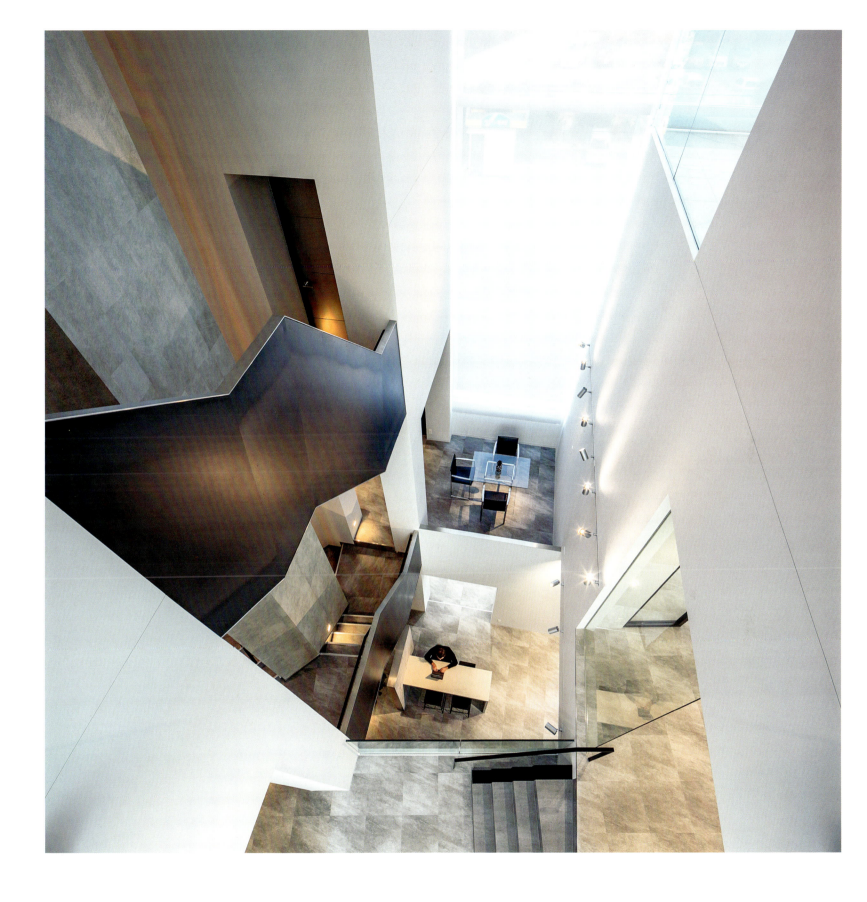

C&C Design Co,. Ltd. Creative Headquarters

Design Company
C&C Design Co., Ltd.

Project Designers
Peng Zheng, Xie Zekun

Project Location
Guangdong, China

Site Area
860 m²

The project is located at the junction of the new city and the old village, where the streets and alleys are separated by only one building. The designer hopes to create a space that fully considers the scale of people and exudes the intimacy of the city. Therefore, the design extracts the characteristics of the multiple symbiosis of nearby streets. Through branch-shaped connectors similar to branch roads, different functional spaces are connected in series to become a traffic core while providing ventilation and lighting for each space. And the forked road leading to the unknown world will also inspire various forms of creativity and opening vision.

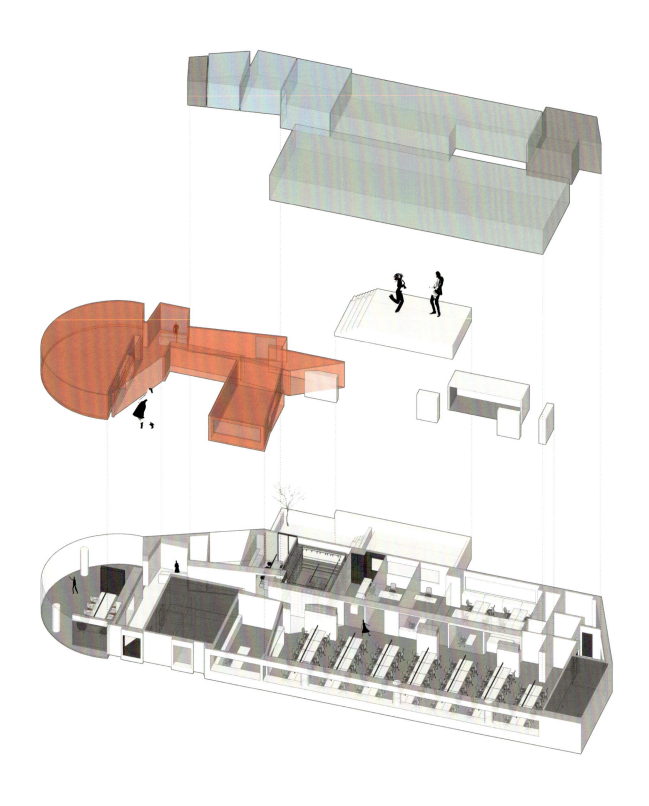

372

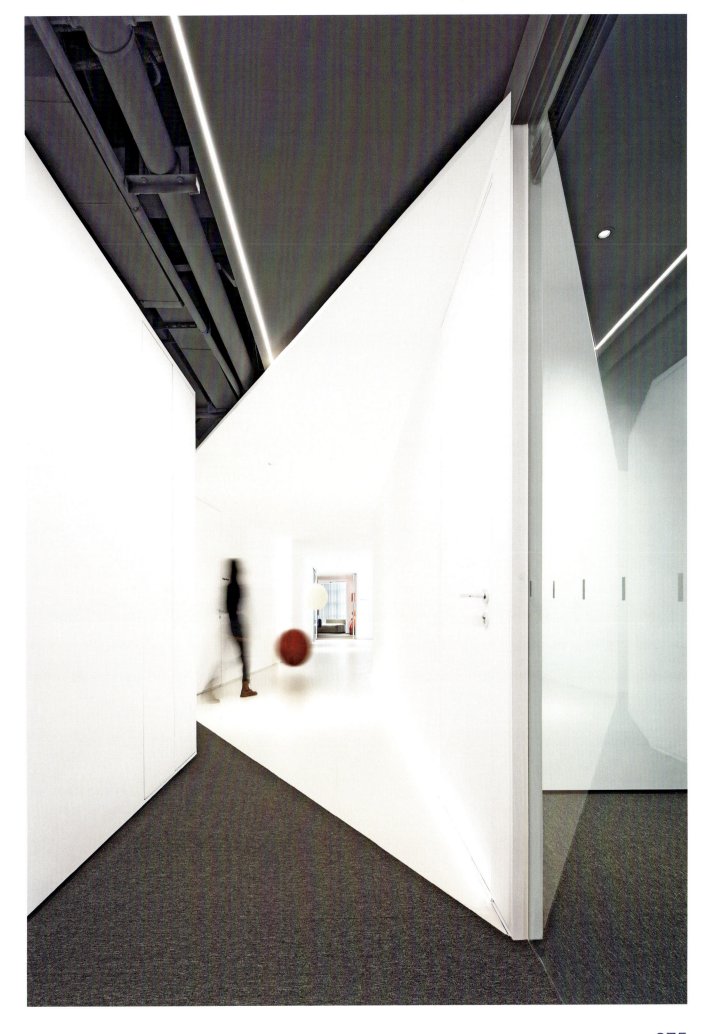

YIJING Architecture Design Studio

Design Company
Shenzhen Yijing Architectural Design Co., Ltd.

Project Designers
He Mincong, Wei Jiaxing, Tang Ting

Project Location
Guangdong, China

Site Area
820 m²

The main purpose of the design is to create "an office in a park, a park in an office". The designer wants employees to come to work in a cheerful mood and can look up to enjoy the trees and bask in the sunshine. The working hours of modern urbanites are constantly extended. But work should not just be boring, we can also shape better life scenes in work and get subtle and delicate feelings and warmth. The integration of work, life, garden and culture and innovation can create a new way of humanistic work.

The original obtrusive pillars "disappeared" through clever design, and are replaced by a space where the sunlight merges with the environment, airflow and light. And through the "design + cultural and creative" model, the online and offline community activities are aggregated to become an innovative space integrating design, exhibition, culture, creative and social interaction, providing a cross-border and mutually integrated platform for the designers.

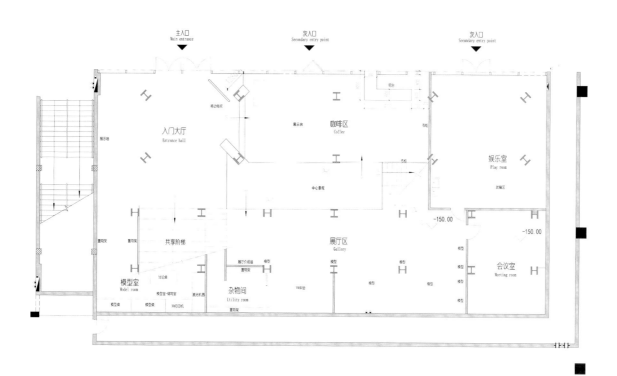
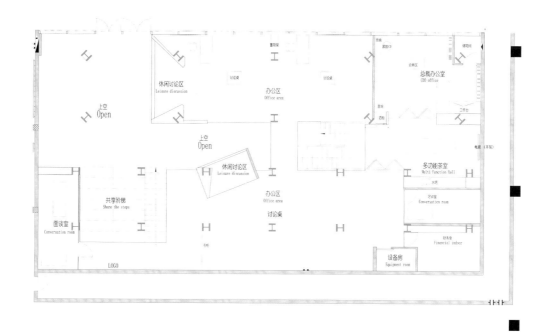

SMALL WORK SPACE

MGY Base

Design Company
teamSTAR

Project Designers
Satake Eitaro

Project Location
Tokyo, Japan

Site Area
125 m²

This project, located in a quiet residential area, is a apparel brand studio. It has an arrow-shaped facade which is very eye-catching. The six-meter-high main floor with huge glass window gives the impression of semi-outdoor space. Openness and comfort eliminates the inherent dreary office image.

Wire mesh, industrial taste lighting, iron fixtures, scaffold and other details represent the secret base the client asked for. It is a third space, pleasant, chic and interesting, that attracts people to meet and work. The designer believes that this will be the future office that people pursue.

Small Work Space

Silver

RMA Office

Design Company
Republican Metropolis Architecture

Project Designers
Ray Wong

Project Location
Beijing, China

Site Area
83 m²

The birth of RMA NEW OFFICE represents an important milestone in the company's design journey. At the same time, this is a redefinition of office space. The design team concentrated on exploring the infinite possibilities of design, combining traditional office needs with different office models to produce a new office space.

The use of mirror reflections on the top of the space gives the space a sense of extension, creating a more dimensional visual effect and breaking the stereotype of the office. Integrating art into simple daily life is the soul of this office.

Designer put a white stainless-steel sphere art installation in the space, just like an interstellar spaceship coming here, full of infinite imagination and mystery.

The quality of a space is that it can support various activities. The versatile space makes work no longer boring.

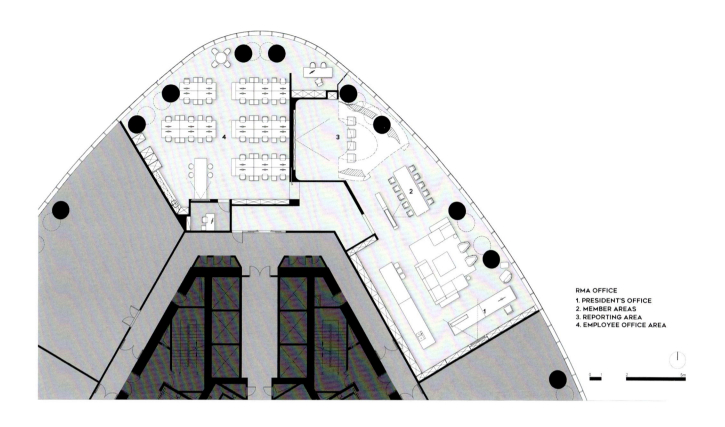

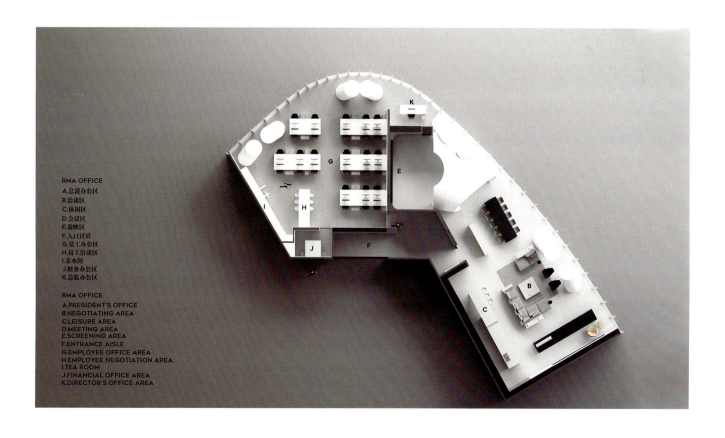

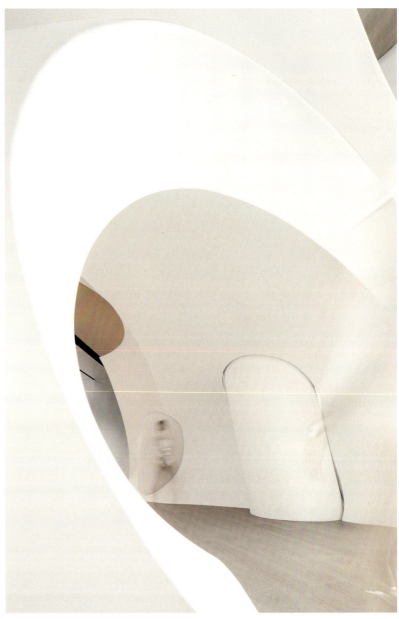

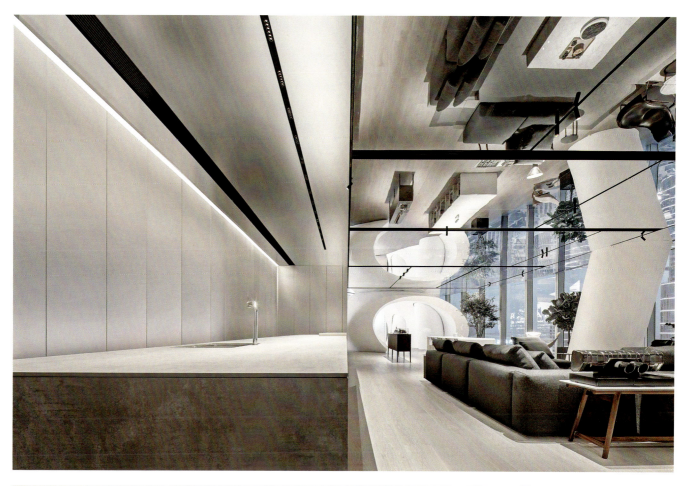

Small Work Space

Silver

Encounter

Design Company
B&T Design

Project Designers
Huang Hanliang, Xie Wenbai

Project Location
Fujian, China

Site Area
170 m²

This project means to leave a quiet place in a noisy street, to create an unexpected encounter, and to meet by chance in the integration of time, art and space. Or office, or gallery, it can be redefined and expressed. Entering the room, walking up or down, everything you see is different. Wherever you go, the feeling will be different. Points, lines, surfaces, and volumes are hidden here and the steps around them float like ribbons, bringing different feelings.

The sinking reception area breaks the traditional layout, which forms high and low level. The staggered platforms visually form a sense of hierarchy and psychologically gives people a sense of intimate. The interior and exterior boundaries are blurred in the inner and outer grey space so that passers-by and interact with interior. Meeting, stepping in and sitting down, everything is telling the integration of man and space.

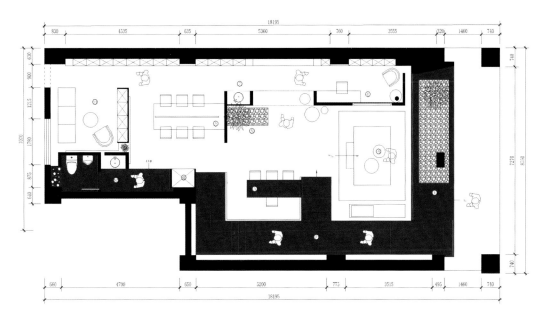

① 灰空间 Grey space
② 楼梯区 Stair area
③ 品茗区 Tea area
④ 洽谈区 Negotiation area
⑤ 景观区 Landscape area
⑥ 总监区 District Director
⑦ 水吧区 Water bar area
⑧ 办公区 Administrative Area
⑨ 文印区 Printing area
⑩ 卫生间 TOILET
⑪ 物料区 Material area

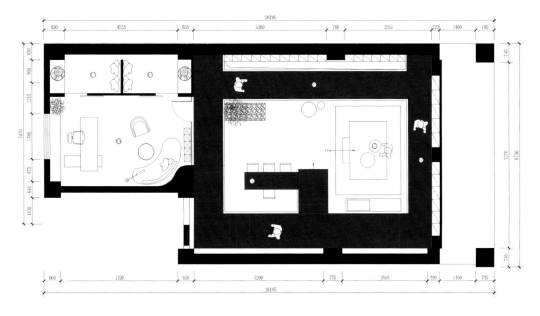

① 艺术画廊&物料 art galleries&Material
② 办公室 office
③ 禅室 meditation room

399

Mastermind JAPAN Office

Design Company
I IN

Project Designers
I IN

Project Location
Tokyo, Japan

Site Area
160 m²

This is a head office design for apparel brand Mastermind JAPAN. The office is about revealing the brand's identity, presented in two different main functions divided within two of the floors of the building they occupy: working space and a presentation environment. Both spaces were asked by the client to have totally different atmospheres. Considering the strong brand's recognition by its fashion society and consumers, which is related to minimal and high craftsmanship, design team approached the design of the interior in two ways — emphasizeing colour and lighting. Black and white are strongly incorporated colours in the core of the client, therefore the designers approached the fashion brand's office as a solid space with bold impression. Its monochrome scheme and the luxury material choices helped creating an impression of juxtaposition between the two floors — one in white and the other one in black.

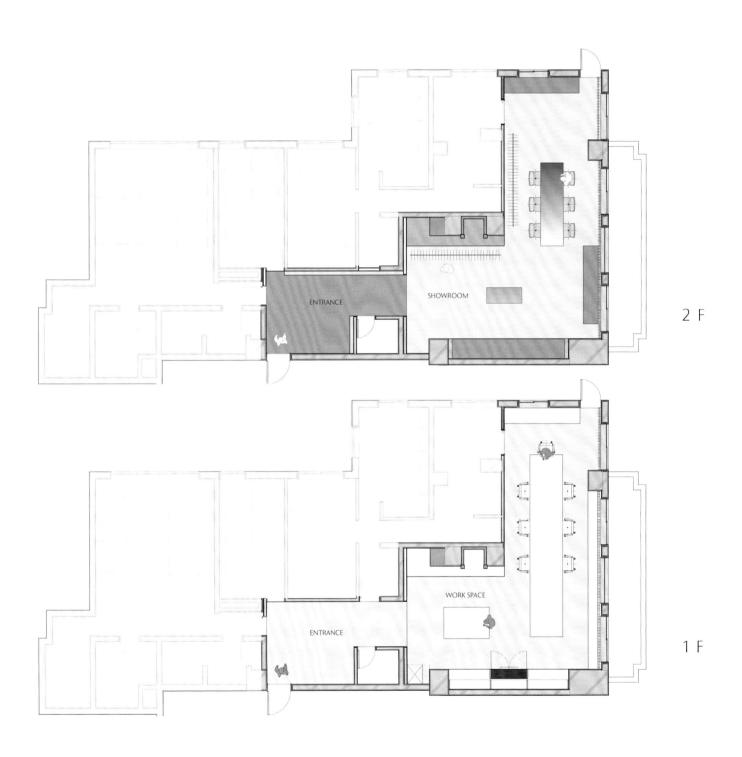

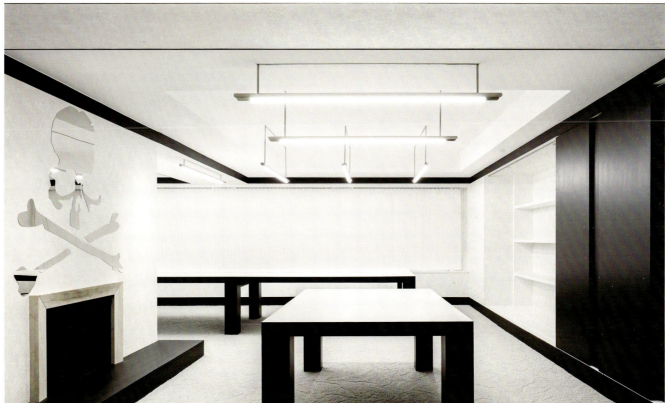

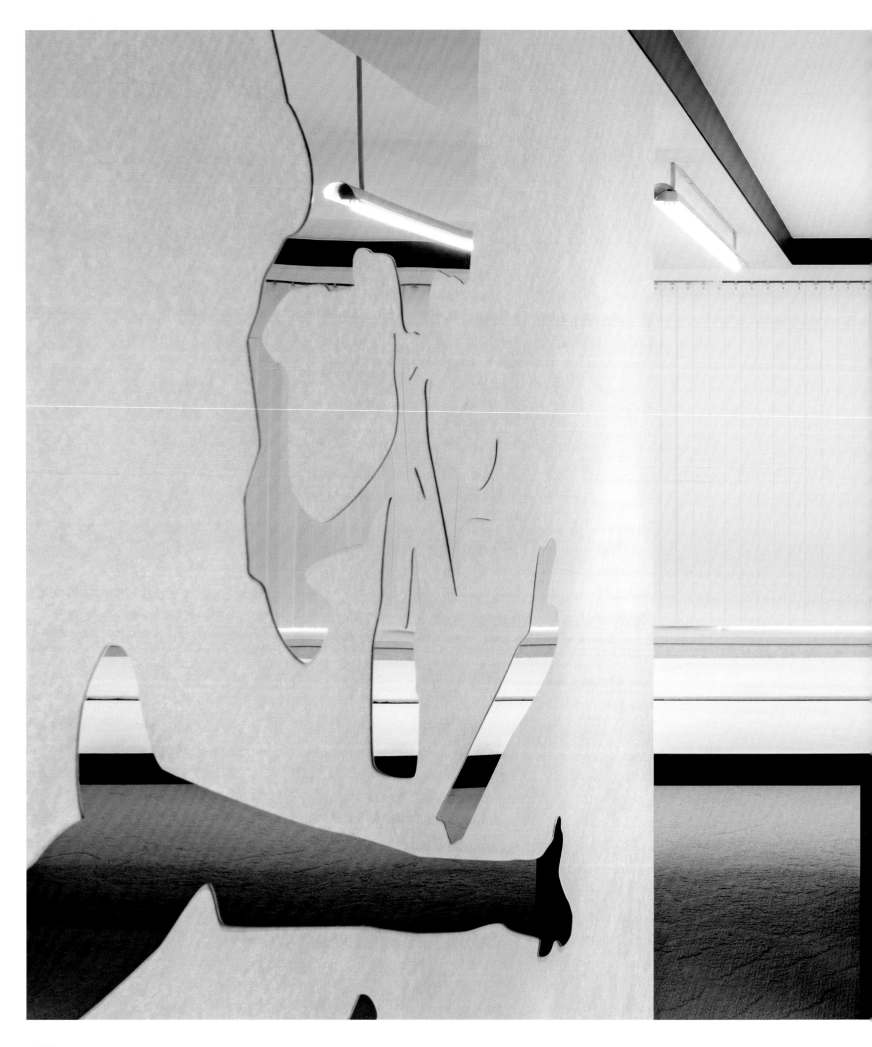

Release

Design Company
Tree House Design

Project Designers
Huang Guofeng

Project Location
Taiwan, China

Site Area
115 m²

Break the encapsulation of an old apartment by introducing the sunlight that sweeps off humidity and darkness. The architectural concrete is the base of a simple and unadorned space, and it preserves the building materials that are covered with traces of the times. Old and new materials complement each other nicely without appearing as a superficial industrial style but with crafted design details to present a layout that embodies work and entertainment.

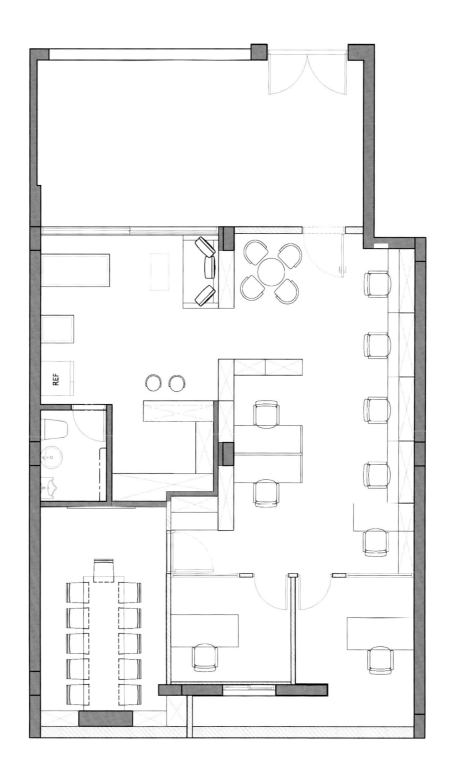

Lou Bai (Liu Bai)

Design Company
Paco Interior Design Limited

Project Designers
Gary Lau

Project Location
Hong Kong, China

Site Area
140 m²

The project is a multifunctional art space for a famous ink painting master, which is both a teaching space and a modern art exhibition space. "Clean and Crisp" is the project's biggest characteristic. The use of crisp white sliding door and mild steel panels can flexibly and functionally change the layout into different spatial planning such as a workshop, exhibition, teaching class, private gathering and gallery. The design here is simple yet stylish and in touch with modern trends.

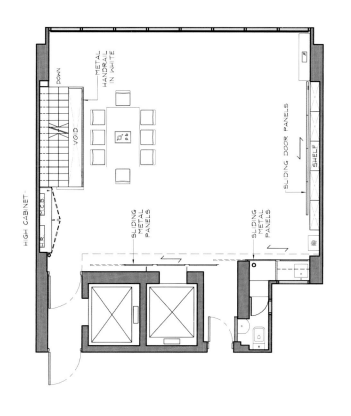

PROPOSED LAYOUT PLAN
9/F SCALE - 1:100 (A4)

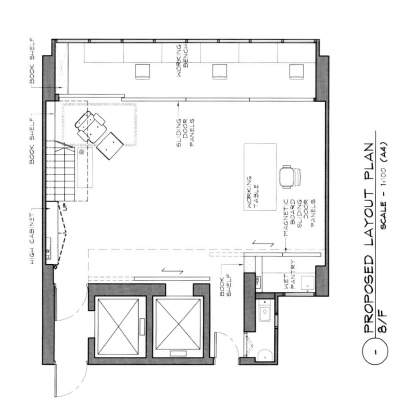

PROPOSED LAYOUT PLAN
8/F SCALE - 1:100 (A4)

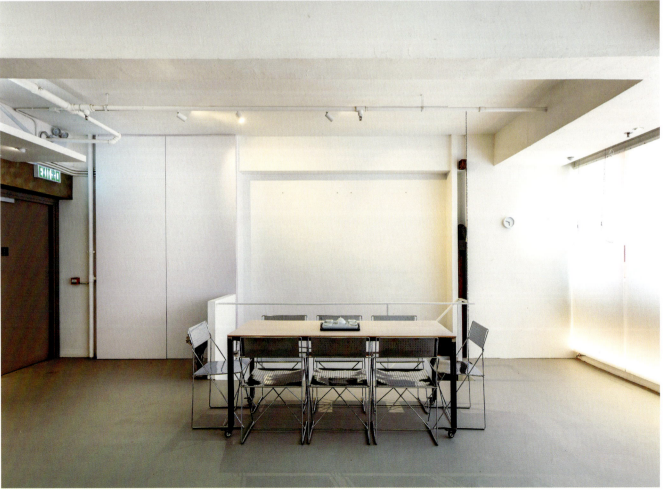

Rebuilding Communication — Tower of Babel

School
The Guangzhou Academy of Fine Arts

Project Designers
Huang Xiaobin

Project Location
China

Site Area
400 m²

In today's society, public space has become an important theme, and this project hopes to introduce urban public space in large urban buildings and use it as the core use scene of the building to build it. Stimulate and guide urban public activities. It is hoped that this space can heal people, reduce barriers and increase communication.

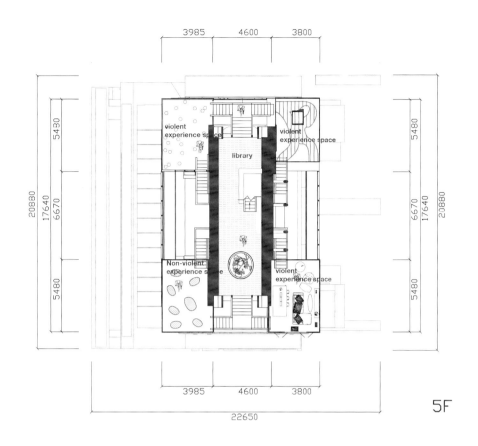

5F

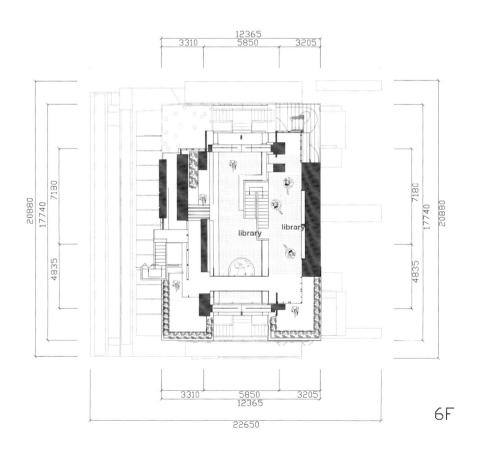

6F

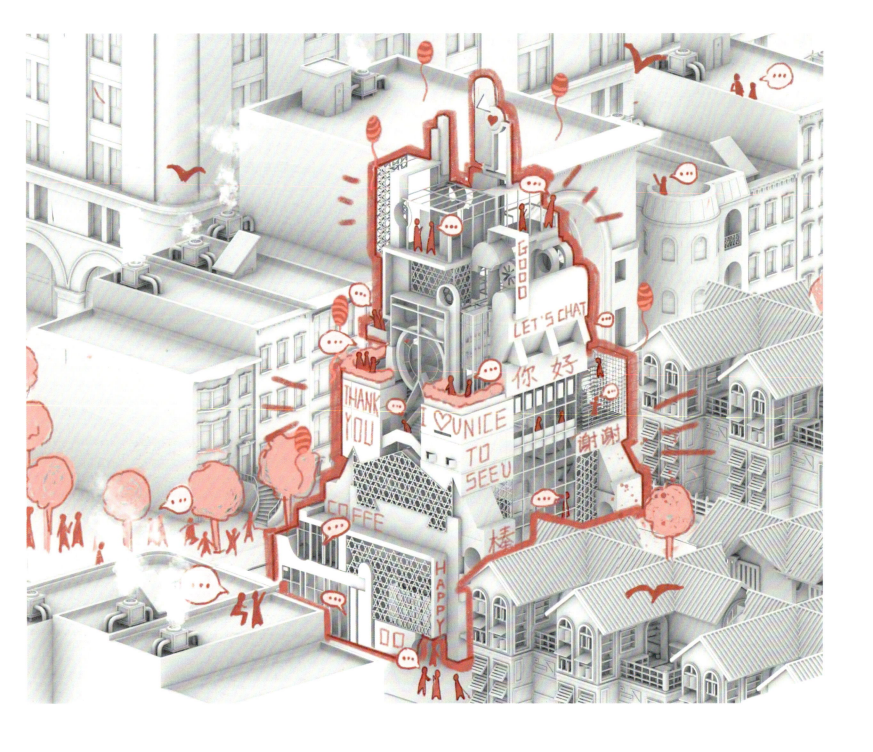

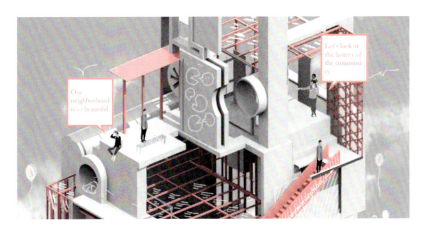

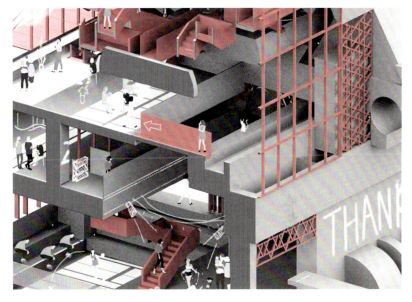

427

Nirvana

School
Hong Kong Design Institute

Project Designers
Tsang Ka Yee

Site Area
3,716 m²

Nowadays, the needs of visually impaired people are always neglected by the society. Therefore, it is designer's sincere hope to raise social awareness towards this issue and assist the visually impaired ones to better grasp the pulse or the latest trend of our society. From designer's point of view, book stores are not limited to sales or the spread of culture, it also represents the image of city. Throughout the design, it has utilised many natural elements and incorporated modern-style and minimalism to embrace the needs of different stakeholders while highlighting the spatial design. It is named after a Buddhist term, "Nirvana". The designer wishes all customers who visit this place can find strength to get back on the horse and embark on a new journey in life.

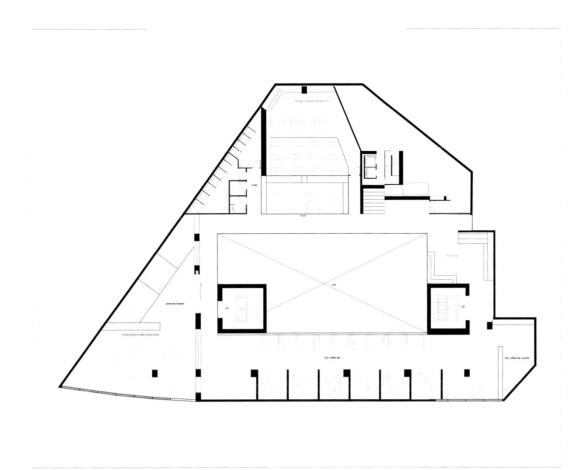
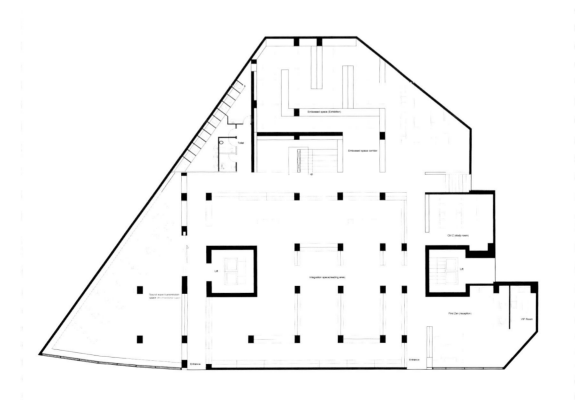

Buddhismscraper in Tibet

School
National Taiwan University of Science and Technology

Project Designers
Chien-Hsun Chen, Tzu-Jung Chin

Site Area
4,780 m²

Buddhismscraper is a skyscraper located above the crater. The crater has formed a lake after years of rainwater accumulation. The skyscraper is a Dzi bead building made of meteorite and Dzi opened the origin of the history of Buddhist civilization. Dzi is a sacred relic worshipped by the Buddhists, and it is passed down from generation to generation as a relic for the Buddha. Buddhismscraper is a place of practice for Buddhists, it's also where Buddhists understand the way of life. Furthermore, learning and practice is an important course for Buddhists and hence this skyscraper is designed for cultivators to reach the highest level through trials and spiritual practice.

Plan

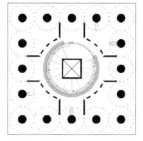
Boat entrance

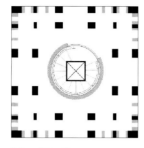
Meditation room

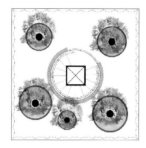
Vertical farming

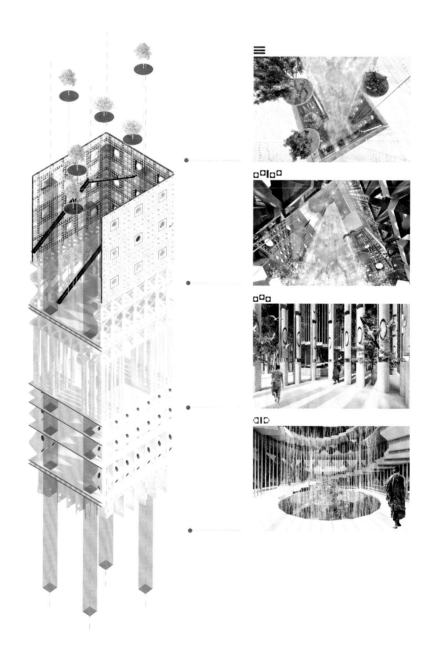

Shell Plaza

School
National Taiwan University of Science and Technology

Project designer
Cheng-Yao, Lin

Site Area
2,820 m²

Located in a forest park in the city, a plaza in the shape of a shell symbolizes the concentration of people's hearts into a pearl. Surrounded by staggered platforms, the flow of space becomes interesting, and the people moving inside seem to be in a 3D maze. In the 3D maze, there are gallery and platforms, hoping to act as a bridge between old and young through outdoor activities and art. The platform area is available for people to drink coffee and read.

CONCEPT

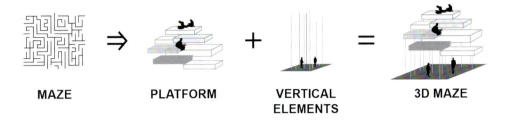

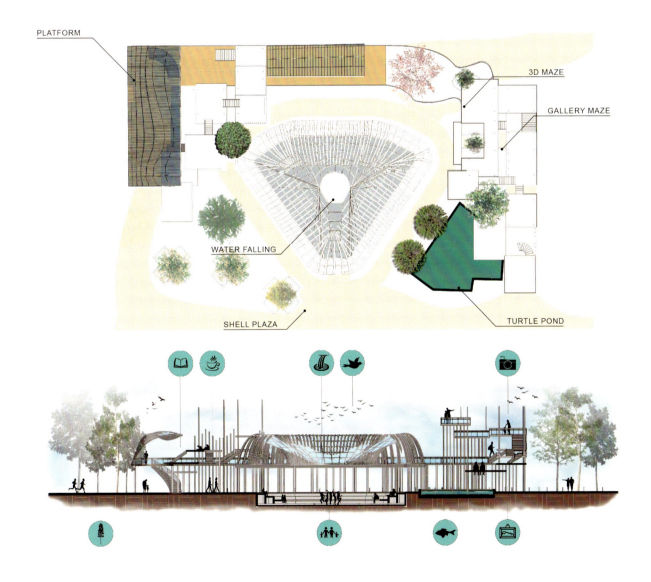

447

ARTPOWER

Acknowledgements

We would like to thank all the designers and companies who made significant contributions to the compilation of this book. Without them, this project would not have been possible. We would also like to thank many others whose names did not appear on the credits, but made specific input and support for the project from beginning to end.

Future Editions

If you would like to contribute to the next edition of Artpower, please email us your details to: contact@artpower.com.cn